What about an algori…what?

By Pablo Gómez Marketer

Copyright © 2024 Pablo Eugenio Gómez Zúñiga
All rights reserved.

The Story

Welcome to a marketing story. This story begins like all others:
Well no, not quite like all others, because this story takes place in a pre-apocalyptic future where a strange force that connects the entire world dominates the great armies.
They call it "The Net."

All the information in the world is trapped in this force, and once The Net has it, it never leaves, staying connected to everything that exists, even when there's no apparent relation.

In this story, there is a good side, but remember this: the good side won't be the hero of the story. The good side is an army fighting against the evil forces of ignorance, boredom, and social disconnection.

The army is made up of millions of soldiers who call themselves creators, artists… well, "entertainers." Within this army, there are many battalions divided by genres, styles, and different rhythms.

They are led by their captain, Melody, who is willing to do anything to protect celestial art, the greatest contraband item. Old as few things that still exist today, it wasn't gold, it wasn't chocolate… it was music. With a legacy of hundreds of years, an endearing, inexplicable, and still immature evolution, music dominated the underworlds in the fight against monotony.

Music was the heart of parties; it accompanied all the dark material in the Net, helped workers survive their long shifts, and was the treasure that almost no one could resist.

On the other hand, there was the bad side, but remember this: the bad side wasn't bad for everyone in this story. The bad side was an army much smaller than the good side but powerful, aggressive, and violent.

This army was made up of soldiers highly trained and dangerous in the dark arts of technology. They possessed extremely advanced and perilous knowledge. Unlike their opponents, they fought the battle without showing their faces, hidden behind an evil machine, operating within the vastness of the Net.

This group was called "The Pirates," but instead of ships, they moved through information; instead of treasures, they had in their possession all the art of music. Instead of a chest, they stored it in small devices capable of holding millions of data points. And instead of treasures, they trafficked in music.

Their leader, Napster Hood, had created the movement decades ago. Every piece of music that touched the Net fell into his hands. He stored it and, through a system called a website, made it available to the rest of the world.

The bad side slowly killed off those soldiers who, after creating a piece of art, saw no return on the value of their work, as the pirates sold the treasure for a few coins paid to them in the form of advertisements... cursed advertisements.

The rest of the world longed for that beautiful art that made their lives better and their days more intense. They adored the creators of music. They gathered in battalions called "Fans," shouting the names of artists and their works with force and intensity.

They sang at parties, bars, gatherings, in their cars, and even at work. They listened to the pieces at full volume on headphones and speakers that had cost more than a few coins... but still, they refused to give even a fraction of their money to their beloved artists.

This is why the rest of the world also loved the pirates, who brought every piece that came to light closer to them for free. It was a strange occurrence; they loved the good, but they also loved the bad. Was the rest of the world caught in the middle of two powerful forces?... NO.

Amidst this war and bloody battles, a new actor was born. A shrewd and cynical merchant who saw an opportunity to make a business. Ek, as the creator of this new movement was known, began to build his own army. It was still smaller than the pirates but even more powerful.

All the soldiers in General Ek's army had one of two characteristics. They were either digital geniuses or possessed fortunes and millions of coins.

Ek had the theory that if they used the same methods as the pirates, charged the rest of the world cheaply, and paid a portion of that loot to the artists, everything would work out. So, he set out to move his army into new battles.

The army, nicknamed Musify, set out to gather all the musical pieces in the Net. For this, they needed significant support from millionaire soldiers and a massive infrastructure where they could store all those pieces, but also with key information such as the creator's name, the album, the genre, and other details.

The idea of General Ek wasn't entirely original. There were other dark places in the Net that delivered music remotely and charged for it. By the time the General had started his project, there were already players like YouTunes, Athena, and Bohemia, to name a few.

These players were just an option to buy music, as was customary before the Net. Before, music was bought on shiny little discs, reflective like mirrors, and housed in small cases that also contained great secrets of the artist, such as the lyrics of their works or personal details.

These players avoided the need to buy the disc and offered it to you through digital magic. But you had to pay the same price. Many armies were eager to buy music this way, but it had not yet reached the majority. Furthermore, many felt that buying such rights was a waste of money, as they received nothing tangible in return, couldn't collect it, and besides, it was available for free.

Both players and pirates had their weaknesses. But there was one common weakness that frustrated the fan armies. The situation lay in the fact that downloading a piece of art or waiting for it to load in the player took time. It turned out that time was an important variable in all the chaos that was unfolding.

For all the above reasons, Musify was focusing on an almost unthinkable achievement. Besides having every piece of music at their disposal, they wanted that when the fans clicked the "play" button, the music would start playing instantly. General Ek's goal was for the time between click and audio to be less than 0.5 seconds.

In addition to this, the Musify army had to work on what was displayed on the screens of the evil machines—fixed, portable, and mobile. So in addition to the music, they had to load information about the artist, album covers, and other details, trying to replicate the experience as closely as possible to the old way of acquiring music. After several attempts and many millions of coins, they achieved it. All the music from the Net was available on Musify, less than a second away.

With this in hand, General Ek still thought the idea wasn't good enough to convince everyone to pay for it. That's when the concept came to him, something that in his mind would break all taboos: charging a single monthly fee for all the music you could consume… yes, that's right… just one coin for all the music you could listen to, no matter where, how, or why.

It sounded like a buffet, but instead of food, it gave you art, and instead of just one moment, it gave you the whole month. General Ek explained to his technological and millionaire soldiers that the concept would attract millions of people and, in this way, the project would be a business like no other, which would also unify the creators with the rest of the world.

Oh, how naive the General had been! The rest of the world didn't understand why they should pay for something that was already available through the pirates. Was it worth a coin just to wait a little less? The creators, upon learning how much they would earn per person who listened to their pieces, felt insulted. Their art was worth thousands and thousands of coins more, and besides, they didn't want to share their pieces in the same place where there was art from thousands of creators.

However, the pirates were being attacked by powerful battalions of art protection. These battalions were composed of a different kind of soldier: lawyers, investigators, police, and movements loyal to the creators. Together, they began to strike strong blows to the pirates. The protection battalions gradually managed to eliminate the sites where art was shared illegally, and they also dealt blows to the pirates' infrastructure, finding their locations with great effort in the vastness of the Net.

This opened up an opportunity for Musify; perhaps it was the right moment to strike with everything. The group of the good, the creators, had their own subgroups, known as "the record labels." These were just as cynical and ruthless with the creators as everyone else, but they operated in an organized and regulated way. If you wanted to be a recognized artist within the industry, you had to join a "label," with all the union requirements that came with it.

The record labels made the creators sign rights contracts in exchange for some coins in advance, and a few more after meeting certain goals. So any decision made by your label had to be accepted, no matter what it was. This is why General Ek, in person, approached several of the record labels in the distant town of Cuesia, a nation contained within the wealthy territory of Ureopa. These labels only had influence in the Free Republic of Cuesia, but it was a start.

After making them see that people had become accustomed to listening to music from the Net and paying little or nothing for it (thanks to the players and the pirates), he managed to make them nervous. He told them he would launch the music project in Cuesia, and that it would generate income either from advertisements or subscriptions, and he would give them a portion of that income, depending only on which songs the people of the nation listened to.

This, combined with the sharp decline of the pirates, the drop in sales of mirror-like discs, and the changes in the habits of the townspeople, managed to get the majority of the powerful labels to sign peace and rights treaties with General Ek, taking the biggest step toward legal, acceptable, and negotiated piracy.

The creators weren't happy, but there was nothing they could do. The General launched his project in Cuesia with two packages: (1) free with ads, and (2) no ads, but with a monthly payment of one coin.

The people of Cuesia understood the first version as a form of "radio," but with the ease of being able to choose the piece and without having to listen to chatterboxes known as DJs. And the second version was seen as a payment for a service, not so much as access to art.

Musify quickly permeated Cuesia, a nation with significant financial power and advanced knowledge and infrastructure in technology. It wasn't surprising that the project had a certain level of success. However, neither advertising revenue nor subscriptions provided enough coins.

The Ureopa territory quickly learned of this event, and people from various towns began requesting it, which helped General Ek to negotiate with record labels that had rights in other nations, such as Angliterra, Francia, Peñasa, and Goruena.

All of these nations had monetary and infrastructural similarities with Cuesia, so the growth of Musify was notable. They even overcame various challenges like the different languages coined in Gomorra, adapting versions of Musify for each nation.

Musify began to appear as a success, but it was only a success on the surface. Behind the scenes, on the business side, it was failing. Ads were paid based on the number of listens, and the subscriptions didn't seem to be enough. The labels and creators were upset about the low payments, the townspeople didn't value the project with purchases, and the pirates… well, the pirates were beginning to disappear.

Musify grew and grew, but it had fewer and fewer coins. If things continued down this path, the situation would deteriorate to the point of making them disappear, and it would happen quickly.

It was at this moment that General Ek had his moment of greatest clarity. The clarity of the business model came to him, not yet with answers or hows, but at least with direction.

For Musify to be viable, it would have to have the majority of the people from the rest of the world, ALL the people from the rest of the world. This would eliminate or overshadow all competition. And what the creators, labels, pirates, or towns thought wouldn't matter.

But how? How to achieve such a feat? General Ek took the first step by thinking: "Something that makes Musify truly unique, truly powerful, truly desirable." But the how was still missing! What frustration!

The General and several of his battalions gathered with thousands and thousands of people from different nations. "What do you need? What do you want? How can I attract you more?" They sought to find key information through an ancient but still relevant method called market research.

After obtaining thousands, no, millions of data points and responses, they managed to isolate the most important ones and present them to all the millionaires who had funded Musify:

- I want Musify to play only music I like continuously, without me having to search song by song or listen to a whole album.
- I want to discover new music, but in the style of the music I already listen to. There are many creators on the Net, and I only know a few.
- I want there to be playlists, something like what we used to call "Mixed Tapes."

The three requests were set in stone as new objectives for Musify's tech team. How? Not yet, but what? That was ready.

One of General Ek's most loyal soldiers approached him with a great idea. An idea that would become the first pillar of an entirely new stage in the art of music: Playlists.

These playlists could be organized by music genre, situation, or even language. For example, by genre, there could be a playlist like "90s Pop," "The Greatest of Hard Rock," "Classical Music," or "60s Classics." For situations, it could be "Latin Party," "Road Trip Music," "Rock for Working Out," or even "Music to Cry To," and each could have a surname like "in English," "in Spanish," or "in Portuguese," for example.

This idea was truly revolutionary. It may not seem so to you because you live in a future beyond this one, perhaps even in a post-apocalyptic future, who knows.

The whole team spent hours and hours planning what these playlists would be like. "They can contain new music mixed with old," "They can change over time," "They can serve as a launch platform for some pieces," "They can have funny, unique, irreverent, or provocative names."

Everyone on the team contributed ideas enthusiastically, with the clarity that the provided information and the new objectives had given them. Playlists solved almost every single one of the three requests from the people.

Musify was losing coins by the day, while the tech team worked 20-hour shifts building this new model, crafting the playlists, integrating the functions into the player, and figuring out the most efficient ways to update all of the playlists.

Once this functionality was ready, it was launched across Ureopa, and additionally, this opened the doors to negotiations with record labels from a distant but powerful nation called United We Stand. This nation was located in a mostly impoverished territory known as Emárica, but they were as large, powerful, and wealthy as any nation in Ureopa, if not more.

The General wasn't entirely unfamiliar with advertising; he charged for it and knew how to handle it. So he used it to announce the new feature all across Ureopa and to pave the way for entry into United We Stand. But he still had an ace up his sleeve, prior to launching the playlist feature: it would only be available to paying subscribers.

What? What's the General thinking? Is he crazy? So much effort, and he won't even use it properly? His army was shocked, nervous, some even voiced their discontent, but the General had his plans.

All the advertising that was launched highlighted the benefit of having access to the playlists if you switched from a free, ad-supported plan to a subscription. The risk was enormous; they could lose everything: Advertisers might doubt them after such an aggressive move, people could get angry for showing them something they couldn't have, everything was on a razor's edge.

Incredibly, the unthinkable happened. Thousands and thousands of people on the Net who were on free plans were switching to paid subscriptions. The playlists turned out to be something they had never had access to before, and they were being used regularly when listening to Musify.

With this success, Musify's finances began to improve, other players were losing ground, and piracy was becoming a thing of the past. However, the users who switched were already Musify users before; the only achievement was convincing those users to upgrade from a free plan to a paid one.

Moreover, there were still multiple ways to acquire music, so people continued spending coins elsewhere, and creators sought alternative sources of income since they were still unhappy with what Musify was paying them.

General Ek's plan was advancing, but still far from achieving total domination of the music and the Net. Even so, this giant step made him feel confident and calm because the map had been drawn: absolute differentiation.

Ek knew that if he continued differentiating Musify, he would dominate the entire world of music, and no force or power on the entire Net would be able to take away his monopoly. While the General was proving to be a genius, he also began to show traces of authoritarianism, dictatorship, and musicide. He shifted from seeking reconciliation to intending to dominate everything… and he was determined to achieve it.

The growing popularity of Musify, the stabilization of its finances, and the steady growth kept both the tech soldiers and the millionaires calm. After many stumbles, confidence in Ek was at an all-time high, and they were willing to work all the hours and invest all the coins in the ideas Ek put forth.

The team had a clear path forward and even some of the goals in sight. However, the next request from their leader would be a major technological challenge, but it made complete sense given the objectives they had set: "Let the users create their own playlists."

Ek recalled how this idea related to "Mixed Tapes," and with this change, which didn't seem very significant at first, it would happen. Each user would not only be able to listen to playlists made by Musify, but they would also be able to create their own "Mixed Lists" to listen to whenever they wanted. The development was slow and frustrating, but ultimately successful. And within this success, there was a happy accident: It turned out that the playlists created by users could be listened to by other users, just like any other playlist on Musify.

This began to pave the way for the final strategy. The ease of creating playlists not only personalized the Musify listening experience to a high level, but also allowed these users, by enjoying the benefit of their own creations, to do a large portion of the heavy lifting that Musify no longer had to do. This was essentially automating differentiated playlists, now truly something that no one else in the world of music had.

As expected, the changes and improvements to the platform resonated quickly with users. The number of users switching from free, ad-supported plans to paid plans was impressive, and Musify's penetration into new nations and territories began to spread. Ek was attacking every territory in the rest of the world.

Unlike previous successes, the inclusion of new users who had never before registered on the platform began to be significant. Personalized playlists from users were spreading by word of mouth, and this started to generate a highly desirable sense of aspiration.

After battling for over six years against all obstacles, understanding the market, and advancing the technology and offerings, the time had come to take a break. The finances were in the green (though there was still no ROI), the tech soldiers were proud, the millionaire soldiers were calm, and the users were satisfied.

There were two steps left to reach where the aggressive, cynical, and ambitious mind of the General was set. And there were still two factors that weren't entirely fulfilled:

(1) The platform's users made up slightly less than 50% of the rest of the world, meaning that creators had other income options and weren't paying enough attention to their relationship with Musify, as the amount paid per play was still too little in the eyes of the artists.

(2) There didn't seem to be an improvement in the number of visits and plays for new or lesser-known artists.

The team decided to return to the greatest strategy that marketing can have, and that had already yielded results: market research. They ran two very targeted studies to answer two equally focused questions, with the second study following the first, based on its results:

(1) Why don't you listen to new artists? The result was similar to the hypothesis but with some interesting twists. The users said they could only listen to what they knew, and that, in reality, with so much new music, they couldn't dedicate time to search and decide who to give a chance. It could be artists, songs, or projects—the possibilities were

many, and even though there was a great desire to discover new things, there was no mechanism to facilitate that option. And,

(2) How could I suggest something you'll like? This second study was an experiment. It was conducted with over 1,000 pairs of people, one pair for each experiment. Individual vs. Individual. They listed the top 100 most-played songs for each person. The pairs with the most overlap in "plays" (meaning they liked the same songs) were matched. In a second step, they separated the songs that weren't in common (meaning one person listened to them, and the other didn't). In the third step, they presented a list of the non-matching songs to the other person (so they could listen to the songs that their match had as favorites, but they didn't).

This final experiment was overwhelmingly conclusive. 98% of the pairs concluded that the music they discovered thanks to their match was mostly appealing, they liked it, and they discovered new artists with styles very similar to what they already listened to. It's worth noting that the overlaps had nothing to do with music genres.

Of the more than 250,000 songs that were "suggested" to the non-matching pairs, over 200,000 were well received. The mental connection seemed so logical that they couldn't understand why it hadn't occurred to them earlier. But let's be honest, without having traveled the path they had traveled, the logic wouldn't have come to them. Marketing is a tool that evolves and matures in conjunction with ideas, processes, projects, and innovation.

Given these results, the clarity of the new objectives to dominate the entire world of music became even clearer: create a system that suggests artists and songs (new or old, famous or niche, local or foreign—regardless of the musical strategy) to each user.

With this goal in mind, they needed to establish a means of delivering suggestions, so the development team considered continuing through playlists. The whole team set out to find that means, eventually proposing two concepts that would be developed together.

The first concept of delivery was based explicitly on the second study: "Personalized Playlists." In each paid account, between 1 and 6 playlists would appear, depending on the user's music tastes, which they would have the freedom to listen to whenever they wanted.

Each of these playlists would contain, let's say, 50 songs: 25 of the user's most played songs and 25 suggestions. To better illustrate this concept, the system would "extract" the 200-300 most-played songs by a user, then extract mini playlists of 25 songs and reclassify them by genre (a piece of data that would need to be filled in by the creator within the platform and approved by Musify). And so, they would have their playlists, which could be called something like Mix of the Day 1 – 6.

By including these 25 songs, the system ensured that the user understood what it was about—they would see songs they already liked, making it a coherent list. Additionally, the user would benefit from a good number of new suggestions.

The 25 songs selected for, say, Playlist 1 would then be cross-referenced with thousands of other Musify users. Again, for illustrative rather than exact purposes, let me explain with a simple example: Let's say the user has listened to Song 1 on Playlist 1 a hundred times. The system would then search for 1,000 people who have that same song in their Playlist 1 with roughly the same number of plays. At this point, the "matching" criterion between the user and the rest would be fulfilled.

Now, the system would search among these 1,000 people (already chosen as matching criteria) for all the songs that are in their original list of 25 but that have NOT been played by User 1. At this point, a second criterion would be met, and they would have a list of, say, 500 songs (that appeal to people who have the same song in the same state as the first).

Next, this list of 500 songs, now identified by the system as the result of appropriate matching criteria, would be sorted from 1 to 500 based on the total number of plays by the 1,000 users who are the subject of similar interest. The top 20 songs, with the most plays, would be added to User 1's Playlist 1. Now, this playlist has 25 songs that the user knows and likes, and 20 suggested songs that the user most likely doesn't know but would probably enjoy discovering and listening to.

So far, we've reached 45 out of 50 songs. For the remaining 5, Musify needed them to be new artists, projects, albums, or releases (or relatively new). To do this, they would use the overall genre criterion. However, there was already a clear understanding that genre alone wasn't enough to suggest or guarantee enjoyment. In other words, just because a song is in the same genre that User 1 listens to doesn't mean it can be recommended with an appropriate level of receptiveness, something that was a priority in their market domination strategy.

The team told the General that the only way to make suggestions with a better success rate would be to cross-reference the genre variable with at least two or three more variables. The challenge was that the databases already existed, and adding classification variables for each song was a Herculean task, which also didn't seem to fit within the team's or General Ek's plans and timelines.

Thus, they set out to think of something that was already within the databases and/or that the system could analyze without needing to "re-feed" the data of each song. Between brainstorming, connections, and available online tools, they concluded that three more variables could be used, although it would require a lot of technological effort—and coins.

They decided (even though these aren't the most reliable variables today) that they would use:

(1) Duration, that is, the system, through simple mathematical operations, would choose suitable song length ranges for each individual, based on the user's most-played songs. This data already existed for each song within Musify.

(2) Tempo, or as we know it better, "the rhythm" of the songs. Tempo is a simple metric that determines how fast a song goes and is measured in beats per minute (BPM). Imagine when you hear a song, and your hand taps the table to the beat. The more taps you make per minute, the faster the song is, and the more BPM it has. For example,

a ballad might have a tempo between 60 to 90 BPM, a pop song between 100 to 130, rock between 110 to 140, and thrash metal can easily reach 220 BPM. This data didn't exist in the database, but it's a classification that doesn't require review—the speed is the speed. So they would incorporate an existing tool to generate the data in the "appropriate language."

(3) Loudness. This translates to something like "noisiness" (though the correct translation is "sonority"). The tech soldiers, with their extensive knowledge of music, had located this variable and identified that it could be found (also using existing tools) within each song. A highly romantic ballad, an acoustic song, or elevator music would have a very low loudness level. On the other hand, a song from the heavy, power, thrash, or death metal genres would have a very high loudness level. This last variable was also totalitarian and didn't require judgment. Among several units of measurement used, the most important is called LUFS (Loudness Units relative to Full Scale). As part of the LUFS formula, factors like decibels, sound pressure level, and true peak are used, so the levels are almost always negative. For example, TV and radio use -23 LUFS, streamers or YouTubers use around -14 LUFS. In other words, the loudness of streamers is higher than that of TV, but it has nothing to do with volume. You could listen to the TV at a volume of 40 and a YouTube video at a volume of 5, and the TV would sound louder, but the loudness would still be higher in the YouTube video.

So, after this brief explanation of the variables, let's return to our plan to conquer the world of music… I mean, Ek's and his team's plan. Using the same logic described earlier to arrive at 45 songs, they would apply the same criteria to suggest 5 new songs, artists, projects, or albums.

To recap a bit, the system would extract parameters from User 1's playlist, which currently has 45 songs, and determine ranges, references, or totals for genre, duration, tempo, and loudness. Assuming their Playlist 1 is a pop playlist, the references would look something like this: Pop / 170 to 260 seconds / 65 to 85 BPM / between -19 and -11 LUFS.

Now, at the height of its powers, maybe in that future where you're reading this story, there are 15,000 song releases every Friday. The platform, supported by the code being developed, would extract the 5 songs that most closely match the four variables of the playlist. And thus, Musify would add to the suggestions the 5 missing songs, which would be new artists, songs, projects, or albums. This way, the 50-song playlist would be a perfect fit for the user, theoretically allowing them to listen to a mix of 50 songs: 25 they love, 20 they didn't know but should like, and 5 new projects that perfectly match their preferences.

All this we've just described was Concept 1 for delivering suggestions. But we still have to look at Concept 2, which is much simpler to both create and explain now that we've delved deeply into the first one.

This second concept would be called "The Station." The hypothetical solution to song suggestions based on user preferences and statistical cross-references was already in place. To be honest, it's not as complex as terms like code, programming, matching, and other buzzwords might make it seem.

This second concept is more about artists than individual songs—mainly in terms of calculation, not delivery. The team had also realized, thanks to all the acquired experience and research, that there seemed to be a significant relationship between an artist's fanbase and other artists. The study also established that when a person repeatedly listens to songs by the same artist, it could correlate with their preferences for other similar artists. For instance, if you frequently listen to Artist POP1, it's likely that you also enjoy listening to Artist POP2.

Thus, the idea behind this second playlist was theoretically riskier, but on the other hand, it would suggest a higher percentage of new songs. The solution was simple—like listening to a radio station that you know you enjoy.

Let's proceed with a scenario to illustrate the idea. Suppose User 1 is a huge fan of an artist called Nadomma. This user has played a large number of songs by this artist. The system's mission would be to once again "extract" these artists for cross-referencing, but this time, it would suggest a playlist called something like "Nadomma's Station."

The first significant difference is that this playlist isn't personalized exclusively for User 1. It's designed for everyone—ALL users—who frequently listen to Nadomma. Within the playlist, you'd find Nadomma's most popular songs, say, about 10 out of 100 songs. The rest would be added through list cross-referencing. That is, once all users who regularly listen to Nadomma have been identified, the system would analyze which other artists those users tend to listen to in addition to Nadomma.

The result would likely be a list of 30 or 40 related artists, such as Jacky Michealson, Princess, Mylie Kinogue, Gady Laga, Hiranna, Spiney Brears, and Bavid Dowie, among others. The system would then select the most popular songs from these mentioned artists and add them to Nadomma's station. Let's estimate about 2 or 3 songs from each artist, out of a total playlist of up to 40 artists.

This playlist, which is more public and aimed at gaining popularity, focuses on ensuring that the user listens to songs that closely resemble the profile of one of their dominant tastes. Of course, it's possible that songs or artists the user doesn't know could appear, but the intent wasn't as strong as with Concept 1. However, the goal was to include recently released songs, with around 4 or 5 included in the playlist. This served two critical purposes: the suggestion of new music, as we've discussed, and the promotion of newer or lesser-known artists by "comparing and equating" them to well-established artists.

These playlists would succeed based on the name and fame of the artist headlining them—in this case, Nadomma. By launching a playlist under her name but with songs from various artists, they achieved broader penetration and reach. Of course, there was a risk that users might dislike some of the songs or find the playlists less appealing.

It's worth noting that the number of songs and the order in which they're added isn't entirely precise. Many details haven't been publicly disclosed yet. Still, for descriptive purposes of ideas, concepts, and projects, I think it serves its purpose.

At this point, General Ek and the Musify team had finally achieved clarity about their next steps. To the General, taking this step would be the final nail in the coffins of those who competed for music distribution on a global scale.

With Musify having entered virtually every territorial market in the world and now holding between 30% and 56% market share in each country, the team set out to write a piece of code—a term that was both trendy and somewhat mysterious: an algorithm.

The way we've come to adopt and use the term "algorithm" makes it sound incredibly complex, and it could be, but not in its original form. An algorithm is simply a computer program or code that reacts in a particular way to various variables. You and I use algorithms every day. When making decisions, for example, you evaluate a series of variables, prioritize, establish a couple of options, and then make a decision. We do this unconsciously, but it's simple.

The algorithm can also evolve over time and consider variables that move consistently. Let's use a soccer player as an example. Upon receiving the ball and knowing their next action is to make a pass, they have to evaluate: 10 teammates, 11 opponents, a referee, the boundary lines, and even the situation in the game (whether they're winning, drawing, or losing). The player makes a decision and passes the ball—sometimes correctly, sometimes incorrectly—but in theory, they had to evaluate: 22 highly mobile variables, 1 limited-mobility priority variable, and at least 2 non-moving variables, like the field's boundaries.

Experts often simplify the explanation to a cooking recipe. There are ingredients, quantities, temperatures, mixtures, times, and in the end, if you follow all the instructions, you'll have a result close to or identical to what was planned from the beginning. This makes the algorithm effective from the perspective of data collection (based on a nearly perfect previous recipe), data organization (translating initial data into a series of steps or instructions), and communication or execution of those steps. These three processes are commonly the foundation of algorithms, not forgetting that complexity must be considered.

I understand if this part of the story feels heavy and confusing, and you may wonder why it's even relevant, but I assure you there's a purpose in explaining that algorithms aren't as complicated as they seem. They're simply the execution of basic math combined with flow processes that we handle every day—only we don't write code or work from a computer.

With that said, the battalion of tech soldiers set out to write the code mentioned earlier. Of course, it was challenging. The size of the input and output databases was enormous. The platform was already written and functioning, so they had to write the code, make it work, execute it, and integrate it into Musify. But in the end, it was just a task that, with the clarity gained and the experience of the team, simply had to be completed.

And so they did!

I'll try to include the steps for writing an algorithm like this in another section of the book, but for now, it's not as relevant.

The launch was gradual. They took cautious steps, not wanting the master plan to fail on a large scale. But in the end, it was incredibly well received. The strangest thing over time was that high-demand users gradually stopped noticing that they were being continuously suggested music, and the functionality began to work naturally. That said, when users switched to another music player or streaming service, the experience felt markedly different—negatively different. Over time, this caused a high level of loyalty toward Musify.

Both first-time subscriptions and upgrades to paid subscriptions increased daily by thousands, maybe even millions, of users, and it was only a matter of time before Musify held more than 60% of the global market. Now, its dominance was powerful, aggressive, and controlling. Ek was achieving what he had sought all along—becoming the only and best option for listening to music with a wonderful experience.

From that moment onward, no one could grow in music distribution except Musify. The recommendation algorithm had been the master strategy that delivered a solid and decisive blow to the entire world of music. Ek had given a great example of perseverance, but above all, adaptability, data-driven decision-making, and the creation of marketing strategies—PURE marketing.

However, at that stage, music creators felt a particular rejection (perhaps even hatred) toward Musify and its leader. The income generated for creators from the playbacks of their songs wasn't satisfying. The payment scheme was based on a total of $3,000 to $5,000 for every million plays, which translates to 3-5 dollars for every 1,000 plays or 0.003 to 0.005 dollars per play. However, the forecast began to show that Musify would only continue to grow, and artists would have to adapt. This situation was also key to the development of this story, as several creators began to develop strategies more aligned with Musify and less with traditional methods. They also started seeking more income through live performances, which, in a way, also benefited this strange world of music.

Not that I agree with the General, far from it. His near-monopolistic dominance and payment policies for creators remain highly controversial within various levels of the industry. However, the force with which he had struck seemed irreversible, so the discussions could continue but with little hope for progress.

The algorithm began to deepen its impact on Musify's user base. People were listening to fewer "albums" and increasingly relying on playlists. The rest of the world seemed to show less interest in album releases and more in singles. Music genres also began to feel the impact, and creators started using formulas related to their play counts on Musify.

At this point, the algorithm had demonstrated its capacity to penetrate the market, its power to drive change, and its strength to keep Musify as the leader, bringing the General to over 70% of the global music market. That's right, 7 out of every 10 song plays in the world were happening on Musify.

The entire team viewed this as a decisive and irreversible victory. However, the platform's entire innovation operation had shifted toward recommendation systems and automation. They were working on what's called

"Machine Learning," or automatic learning. So, as the next step, they developed two highly specific and deeply personalized playlists for each user (meaning unique playlists for each person). They would be named something like "New Stuff Finder" and "Musical Discovering."

Both playlists had the goal of suggesting new music to users. They would use the same mathematical models and cross-referencing that had led the algorithm to total success in previous steps. The first playlist would contain ONLY the week's new releases. In other words, the platform would select, from among all the releases, the 30 songs closest to the user's listening patterns, offering them as fresh, relevant, and coherent music. The second playlist would do something similar but focus exclusively on music that had been in the market for at least two years. Its goal was to suggest music that already existed but that the user might not know.

It goes without saying that everything continued to be an unstoppable success. The level of understanding they had of their users was astonishing. The last innovation they made wasn't a new idea but a substantial improvement to their models, adding a much larger number of variables to the platform's analysis to categorize and suggest music. With Musify's broad reach and extensive learning, they opened the door, and it's said that in the dark corners of the web, the following variables are used to understand you, categorize you, project your tastes, and suggest music… assuming you're a Musify user:

- **Music Genre** (already explained)
- **Duration** (already explained)
- **Tempo** (already explained)

- **Loudness** (already explained)
- **Danceability**: How "danceable" the songs are
- **Energy**: The intensity or "power" of the songs, in a combination of tempo, genre, and loudness.
- **Valence**: A spectrum that moves between Happy and Sad and everything in between.
- **Acousticness**: How acoustic (or not) a song is
- **Instrumentalness**: The number and types of instruments used in the songs the user listens to most.
- **Key**: The musical key of the songs the user listens to, such as C Major, F Minor, or G Sharp.
- **Liveness**: This spectrum ranges from a traditional studio track to a live concert recording. However, there are interesting gray areas, like a band that records a song in the studio but plays all together, or a singer who records their vocals in one take.
- **Speechness**: The percentage of the song that includes lyrics (words).
- **Song Titles**: Using AI models (not just for this variable, but many of the others as well), it's possible to classify the types of titles people prefer.
- **Artist Metadata**: Here, participation from the creator is required to upload information, in addition to the data generated for each artist on the platform.
- **Mode**: Whether the person prefers major keys, minor keys, sevenths, or jazzy scales.

The evolution of the model was already impressive. Imagine the depth—if we go back to the beginning of the algorithm, it was based SOLELY on the coincidence of song preferences between individuals. Now, with 14 variables (and others unknown to mere mortals), Musify's business muscle had grown immensely powerful.

The return on investment for the millionaire soldiers was now a reality, the profits were enormous, the machine's evolution was constant, the market dominance was almost monopolistic, the loyalty of users was absolute, and the acceptance by creators (although resigned) was becoming evident in their actions.

Ten years after its creation, Musify went public, raising an enormous amount of capital to continue its expansion and crush any would-be competitors. With this capital, two years later, they acquired content creation companies (like podcasts, music, and video), allowing them to create exclusive content and diversify the platform's offerings further. Within less than a year, they also dominated the podcast market globally.

By the time they reached 15 years, they had started creating tools for content creators. Their operation was maintained to improve the user experience and interface, and to continuously develop strategies that would prevent any dangerous penetration by new players in the streaming market.

They continued releasing highly popular features, such as the "Musify Pack," which roughly provides:

- **Most-listened songs and artists**: A list showing the songs and artists you listened to the most during the year, letting you reflect on your musical preferences.
- **Favorite genres**: A breakdown of the musical genres you listened to the most, highlighting the diversity of your musical taste.

- **Minutes listened**: The total amount of time you spent listening to music and podcasts on Musify over the year.
- **Personalized playlists**: Based on your listening habits, Musify creates custom playlists that reflect what you enjoyed the most during the year.
- **Share on social media**: Presented in an attractive visual format, users can easily share their listening preferences with friends and followers on social media.
- **Comparison with previous years**: If you've used Musify for several years, you can compare your current listening habits with previous years.

It seems that Musify will continue to dominate the music world for many years. The ethics and moral character of General Ek will remain a topic of debate. No one knows for sure whether he created a better or worse world for music. Personally, I still think it's not better, and it's morally questionable, especially for the creators. But… wouldn't you want to be a General like him?

Pablo Talks

I must say this story really fascinated me, both when I first heard it, when I delved deeper into it, and now that I've written it from a different approach. There are few things that strike me as "pure marketing" that aren't traditional. Traditional marketing tools will always help us create and move forward—things like logos, packaging design, websites, etc. But this was a strategy that completely stepped away from tradition, creating something within an existing something, to "disrupt" the market.

I want to emphasize here that I firmly defend the notion that marketing equals sales, plain and simple. To me, if it doesn't sell or help to sell, it's not marketing. In other words, when conducting market research, the results must help us generate data that, in turn, support specific actions that lead to sales: improving the product, service, customer care, sales channels, communication, listing benefits... there are countless ways data can help us.

Now, let's analyze the situational context of the story. The idea arose in what seemed like a market opportunity, where there was destabilization and no apparent solution. However, when you take a cold look at it, the idea was bad, at least in the sense that it was used as the sole market entry weapon, but it wasn't unique—similar, even identical, products already existed.

It's true that the way it was marketed had originality in the concept of a monthly subscription for all the music you could consume, but again, when viewed from a global perspective, there was nothing stopping other platforms from changing their model to this one. They didn't because they already had agreements with record labels and rights holders, and their business models were at least functional (though I can't say if they were profitable). Plus, shifting to a "Musify" model seemed like a colossal task. By the time they recognized Musify's differentiators, the race was practically over.

I know there will be readers who say, "I know of other platforms," "Amazon has one," and so on. But the reality is, they're fighting day by day in a market that is now monopolized. Musify holds 46% of the GLOBAL market, with up to 60% in certain niches. And they don't have more because there are barriers like antitrust laws or refusal of entry into certain nations or territories. Additionally, this 46% includes ALL streaming, meaning it accounts for competing platforms, hybrid sites (like TuTube, which is also used for music), digital radio stations, artist-specific pages, fan club pages, related markets (kids who don't pay), exclusive mobile players, and so on.

To give you an idea, it's estimated that there are just over 500 million premium (paid) accounts on any streaming service used for music. Of those, Musify accounts for 236 million.
We also need to reassess the fact that around 1.6 billion people globally listen to music via streaming (this seems low, but when you eliminate markets like the elderly, babies, those without internet access, people in poverty, the huge number of people who listen through other

people's accounts, and so on), and roughly 40% of Musify's accounts are "Double" or "Family" accounts.

By making a quick calculation, let's assume 20% are double accounts and 20% are family accounts (this is unverified data). This gives us a distribution that looks something like this:

- 142 million individual accounts with 142 million listeners
- 47 million double accounts with 94 million listeners
- 47 million family accounts with 180 million listeners

This totals 416 million people within Musify's premium accounts. Additionally, they have about 350 million free (ad-supported) accounts, of which an estimated 295 million are active. It's also calculated that there are roughly 1.7 people per account (meaning accounts are shared), giving around 500 million listeners for ad-supported accounts.

In my simple, quick, and admittedly reckless math, we can be sure that the actual number of users is around 915 million people globally. This would give Musify an estimated 57% TOTAL GLOBAL market share, establishing it as the undisputed leader and dominator… and it's still growing.

Recapping, a product was created based on a misreading of a market opportunity. They then tried to differentiate it with features that weren't true differentiators and were already covered by the competition. Their only initial differentiator was a monthly subscription concept that did not adequately consider the cost/payment to the "suppliers."

Up to this point in the summary, it seems like a story of failure, but then came the key step to building a different path: the algorithm. As a concept, it really means nothing—it's a programming tool used as a means to achieve the real end: personalization of service and absolute differentiation.

The blow was so direct that not only did it rescue the business, the investment, and the concept, but it also turned them into absolute and undeniable leaders in a highly complex global industry. Its effect was so strong that they now threaten to gradually eliminate more competitors, taking almost the entire pie—so long as they don't make any mistakes, there's no mass exodus of artists, and no competitor comes up with an equally radical and effective idea.

In my experience, most great ideas or key market leadership changes occur under unfavorable circumstances. It seems that negative situational positions have something to do with the fact that, from an undesirable or unfavorable situation, the key to greater success emerges.

I'm not saying that ALL ideas have to go through this phase. Nor am I saying that ALL unfavorable situations bring out the best in people. You also have to consider a third factor that, in my opinion, is just as critical: a winning mentality. A person with this mindset usually has some interesting mental traits, and with a positive, winning personality, come qualities like patience, perseverance, grit, and, today's buzzword, resilience.

From my own observations, I've noticed that when a series of coincidental steps in these kinds of situations occur, it leads a highly driven person to feel trapped or cornered, and they say you never know what a wild animal can really do until it finds itself in such a situation. If Musify had "hit" from the beginning, I'm sure it never would have reached that level of differentiation as a product/service, nor would it have anywhere near its leadership position. It might have been a business in the black, but fleetingly, before fading away. That's what happened to other major companies with very similar products in the same industry.

Now, I'd love to move on to the "why should I care?" part. Throughout my career, I've seen many things, including that when there's room for growth and development within a company, there's an entire world ready to be conquered. Along with that, I've become passionate about and studied the sales techniques and strategies that are often key indicators in the stories of practically every successful company.

Through this, I've detected that the most "mind-blowing," explosive, and globally recognized strategies are transferable to, once again, practically any company, product, or service. What's Pablo getting at with all this rambling? You could apply all the strategies I'll explain in the "Marketing Tales" book series to your business. If you've read the first book, *What Are Your Fries and Big Drink?*, you'll see I provide examples and processes that can be almost immediately applied to sales processes in most businesses.

I just talked about my vision of the cornered animal. Wouldn't it be great to never find yourself in that situation, but still react the same way and achieve the same results? Imagine if I present you with 12 highly successful and differentiating strategies, of which 6 or 7 could be applied to your business or the company where you work. Nowadays, there are few people who do this. They confine themselves to their own processes and methods to create strategies that will somehow need to be "tested" in order to fine-tune them, always with the possibility that they may never succeed. My invitation, with these small (but lovingly crafted) books, is for you to start creating products, services, packages, and sales strategies based on objectives, forms, and methods already tested by others—who have had to suffer a lot to succeed.

The goal is not to copy. That happens every day. The idea is to appropriately translate the concepts and methodologies, extract them, bring them down to earth, organize them, and then apply them in an intelligent and aggressive way. In this case, we're talking about an algorithm (it's even in the book's title). However, I don't advise you to create an algorithm—unless it applies, then go ahead. What's attractive here is understanding the outcome achieved through that mathematics.

The moral of this story is NOT in the tool, technology, or math itself. It's in the fact that a business differentiated itself through personalization and offers EACH individual something relevant, in the right way, at the right time, making them feel like it's tailored specifically for them. This approach has the power to lead an industry where, at first, it was just another fish in the sea.

If we look closely, the product never changed. I mention this because, when I present these topics, my clients often say, "But making new products is extremely difficult." I completely agree! The key lies in changing the WAY you deliver the product to your customer. That is what can lead to a company's success.

So, the songs didn't change. The project was built on the same music that already existed, and of course, on new releases too. But what I mean is, no one had to change the main product, the song, for the project to advance. The artists, albums, and genres didn't need adjustment. The service—music streaming via the internet—wasn't a factor either, as it already existed. I'll say it again, the difference was in HOW the music was delivered to people.

I don't want to delve too much into the ethical aspects of the project in this book. I understand that it's not desirable, advisable, or plausible. But it's hard to ignore the undeniable success of the concept.

Musify, as we've called it throughout, teaches us that we must know our customers well and have mechanisms (whether traditional, modern, technological, or even outdated) to truly gather data about them. We need to know them—not just better, but MUCH better than we do today. There's no personalization strategy without that mechanism in place, and as will be established later in this book, when we explore the 10 steps to apply it yourself.

However, it also teaches us that simply knowing them is not enough. We have to be empathetic and visionary. We must step outside the box, and without necessarily thinking of new products that only complicate our lives, apply TRUE MARKETING in all its glory. Personalizing the way we communicate and sell to our customers.

I know that, depending on the type of business, the nuances can be almost incomparable in both number and complexity. But that's where we have to break out of the same mindset that has been guiding us until now. Let's go to extremes.

Let's talk about a business that has few, but large, clients. Once you establish the mechanism, you need to devote enough time to understanding the uniqueness of each client and making a presentation that makes total sense to them. Yes, it will take time, but if every client is valuable to you, then invest some time to make that sale.

On the other end of the spectrum, maybe you're selling "fries and a large drink," food perhaps, in a big chain that is financially supported by mass sales. Well, maybe we need to make use of some technology, which isn't all that complex. Gather basic customer data and their purchasing behavior, for example, and use platforms to build messages—yes, even an email! Maybe that's enough.

I'll illustrate with an example, although a fast-food company might argue. Let's use Paty as an example. Paty has a card, app, code, or whatever, which she uses to pay and get a 5% discount on every purchase. Paty visited the burger joint 10 times last year. Of those 10 visits, she ordered Burger #3 eight times. She ordered curly fries seven times. She ordered diet cola on all her visits. Now we have that information, along with her phone number, email, or any contact method she provided when receiving her code.

What do you think happens when Paty receives an email that says: "Burger #3, curly fries, and diet cola for $9.99—now $6.99"? The impact will be far greater than if she received the same email promoting the usual triple combo offered at every branch. It's highly likely that this type of incentive will get Paty to visit 13 or 14 times a year instead of 10. Of course, there will be people who won't visit any more than before. But what if this strategy works with 100,000 Patys? That strategy could lead to an additional 300,000 to 400,000 sales next year.

I KNOW! This loyalty program stuff is old news, blah blah blah. The loyalty program is the mechanism. We need to understand that the difference isn't in the mechanism itself. The difference lies in the company's ability to deliver personalized messages to its customers. Paty might think, "Wow, they really know me," or maybe, "How funny, just what I like," or she might not say anything at all! That doesn't matter—what matters is that she goes.

Even if Paty doesn't say a word, this kind of action lodges itself quickly and deeply in people's subconscious. These types of messages are what gradually build customer loyalty and brand recognition. And if we have the intelligence and planning to change that offer every time we detect changes in Paty's behavior, it will serve us even more.

These examples range from black to white, but every shade of gray must have its own application. These books aren't written with the goal of "selling smoke" or offering "magical solutions." My goal is to create not just awareness, but mental clarity so YOU can generate the right marketing strategy. I know I mentioned marketing, but to me, there's no purer marketing than this.

One of the things I love doing when I'm creating commercial or marketing strategies for my business or my clients' businesses is engaging in empathy exercises. Assuming we agree on applying this specific methodology to our plan, we bring it down to an almost staged level. For example, I'd ask my client to tell me the 3 or 4 things they consume most related to the nature of their product (entertainment, food, business, etc.). Then, we'd both force hypothetical situations related to those businesses, but IN TERMS OF my client.

Let's break it down into simple terms, as that paragraph was a bit aggressive. Suppose my client works in the entertainment industry. I'd ask them what the 3 things they consume most in that area are. Let's say they say going to the movies, watching series, and going out to eat with family. From there, we'd start talking about brands—perhaps City Cinemas, TVFlix, and Taco King, for example. The exercise is about what these 3 brands could offer the client that would be personalized, something they'd value enough to continue consuming, consume in larger quantities, or create loyalty beyond the traditional.

The exercise will likely produce ridiculous results or funny ideas. Maybe a concept that seems applicable, or suddenly, a million-dollar idea. But the point isn't to generate feasible ideas for businesses that aren't the client's. The idea is to break through the mental barriers we all have and get into a "mood" that helps us create an entire system that ultimately personalizes our communication and sales approach. That's where the gain is. I'll leave you with that thought, as a side note amidst all the chaos.

In the end, and as a bit of a summary, I believe what we should take away from this story is that differentiation and personalization can make us stand out against any competition, without ever forgetting that business IS a race—a race of time and speed. Why do I frame it this way? Because any other platform could apply the same personalization methodology that Musify did, but it would be a futile effort—that race has already been run and won. Timing was a key element.

On the other hand, there's the analysis of speed. In other words, we must act quickly to plan and execute—though not at the cost of compromising execution quality. Let's remember that the business world is highly permeable, whether through employees, trials, or simply because the information is somehow out there for everyone. I've already experienced it with a couple of clients—due to their infrastructure, budget, and limited company flexibility, when they began testing strategies, they inadvertently "informed" their competitors of their intentions. And what happened? If the competition notices, thinks it's a good idea, and has a larger budget and better infrastructure, they'll take the idea and implement it before you do.

If you've ever seen my videos on Instagram, you'll know that I'm a strong advocate for SEO (organic positioning on Google) as the primary communication tool nowadays. To rank on Google, you must follow a "checklist of requirements" that the search engine itself establishes, and it applies to everyone. When I offer SEO packages to my clients, more than one has asked, "What happens if we all do the same in the industry, if we all meet the requirements? Who comes out on top?" As frustrating as it might sound, the one who gets the top position is the one who does it first.

Later, we'll talk about the necessary steps for you to apply the "Musify strategy" to your business or venture. But I want to emphasize that one of the most challenging, yet essential, aspects of this and many other strategies is the ability to deeply understand your customer. If you want intelligence to be a core part of your sales strategies, you must find ways to deeply, consistently, and accurately know your customers.

If, for some reason, you don't have ANY suitable mechanism to know your customers today, I suggest you plan it in two stages, which for me, are always key:

1. **A comprehensive market research study.** This should include competitor analysis, industry perception, buyer personas, customer satisfaction, and at least one digital study.
2. **A MAINTAINED mechanism for gathering customer information.** This could be as basic as a biannual survey or as complex as an autonomous loyalty plan.

If you manage to create the necessary channels that provide clear, deep, and timely information, you will have half of this and many other strategies lined up to help grow your sales.

The Exercise

WARNING: If you're not interested in applying this strategy now, and you're not a numbers enthusiast, skip this section. It's informative but dull.

Let's look at some illustrative (although percentage-based) exercises to help understand the behavior of these strategies. We will analyze data from approximately 20 years, considering the project's start. I'll divide the story into five phases that I find significant and distinct. Each is marked by an event that triggered a fundamental change in the project:

1. **Investment Phase**: We'll discuss this briefly. It took place from 2004 to 2007.
2. **Launch Phase**: This phase is characterized by limitations in efforts and project vision, from 2007 to 2010.
3. **Differentiation Phase**: Musify begins to distinguish itself, although not entirely, from other competing services between 2011 and 2015.
4. **Breakthrough Phase**: This is where complete differentiation occurs, thanks to personalization via an algorithm, between 2016 and 2018.
5. **Consolidation Phase**: Musify simply had to maintain its position and grow until today, between 2019 and 2023.

The last data I have is from 2023, but as of 2024, Musify is still the undisputed leader.

Phase 1: Investment.

There isn't complete clarity about the exact amount invested, and figures vary in books, series, and reports.

However, experts generally agree that the initial total investment was about $5M USD. There could be significant variations in these calculations, as in the "official" series, they infer it was at least $20 million. All figures are in millions of U.S. dollars.

2004-2007

- **Strategy**: Initial investment
- **Market Reaction**: N/A
- **Differentiator**: N/A
- **Territory Covered**: N/A
- **Number of ad-supported accounts**: N/A
- **Number of premium accounts**: N/A
- **Total accounts**: N/A
- **Average monthly revenue per ad account**: N/A
- **Average monthly revenue per premium account**: N/A
- **Approximate total monthly revenue**: N/A
- **Approximate annual revenue of Musify**: N/A
- **Profit/Loss**: -$5M USD
- **Investment Status**: -$5M USD

Phase 2: Launch.

The development and investment phase took much longer than expected, and speculation suggests it cost far more than generally acknowledged. But the real delay was due to failed negotiations to secure music rights and establish a supply chain for the project. Musify was always intended as a global idea. Its creator and the initial investors had experience with projects that had permeated without geographical limits. However, the issue of rights forced them to negotiate with the local label in Sweden to launch at least the beta test there and not get stuck without making any progress.

In reality, the first three years were not insignificant. By year two, they were in the UK and Spain, and by the third, they were practically across all of Europe. The initial growth and adoption of the technology were supported by the fact that it had been developed in Sweden, but more importantly, the entire geographic zone had much greater infrastructure and socioeconomic standing than most other global territories.

One of the most curious facts about the story is that, at the beginning, Musify earned much more per account than it did later. This is because the competitiveness and purchasing power of their initial territory were much higher than, for example, Africa or Latin America.

Contrary to what the story says (which was slightly altered for dramatic purposes), the early years had no ad-supported accounts, leaving Musify reliant entirely on premium accounts for revenue. Although their territorial penetration was rapid and substantial, their market share was still low. For example, when they were available across all of Europe, they only had 1.5 million accounts. Considering that Europe has more than 700 million people, that figure was still very low. In terms of market share, they had about 0.9%.

By 2010, accumulated losses had reached $72 million USD, with no quick turnaround in sight. Here's an analysis of the general market behavior, company performance, and finances:

2008

- **Strategy**: Launch
- **Market Reaction**: Curiosity
- **Differentiator**: Playback speed
- **Territory Covered**: Sweden
- **Number of ad-supported accounts**: 0
- **Number of premium accounts**: 211,000
- **Total accounts**: 211,000
- **Average monthly revenue per ad account**: $0
- **Average monthly revenue per premium account**: $8
- **Approximate total monthly revenue**: $1,688,000
- **Approximate annual revenue of Musify**: $20,256,000
- **Profit/Loss**: -$7,697,280
- **Investment Status**: -$12,697,280

2009

- **Strategy**: Expansion
- **Market Reaction**: Interest
- **Differentiator**: Speed and catalog
- **Territory Covered**: Sweden, UK, Spain
- **Number of ad-supported accounts**: 0
- **Number of premium accounts**: 419,568
- **Total accounts**: 419,568
- **Average monthly revenue per ad account**: $0

- **Average monthly revenue per premium account**: $8
- **Approximate total monthly revenue**: $3,356,544
- **Approximate annual revenue of Musify**: $40,278,528
- **Profit/Loss**: -$14,097,485
- **Investment Status**: -$26,794,765

2010

- **Strategy**: Platform growth. More launches
- **Market Reaction**: Rapid adoption
- **Differentiator**: Expanded catalog
- **Territory Covered**: Europe
- **Number of ad-supported accounts**: 0
- **Number of premium accounts**: 1,433,833
- **Total accounts**: 1,433,833
- **Average monthly revenue per ad account**: $0
- **Average monthly revenue per premium account**: $8
- **Approximate total monthly revenue**: $11,470,664
- **Approximate annual revenue of Musify**: $137,647,968
- **Profit/Loss**: -$45,423,829
- **Investment Status**: -$72,218,594

Phase 3: Differentiation

This part is especially interesting to me because it's when they realized they needed to differentiate through personalization, but they couldn't fully execute it effectively. However, their other differentiation strategies—like launching ad-supported accounts, expanding their catalog to include artists worldwide, releasing a mobile app, and their **Connect** project—did create significant behavioral shifts globally.

They were still burdened with the financial pitfalls common to most startups. While sales increased, so did losses. This is typical for tech companies disrupting industries, where the target market demands the service, but the costs of covering that demand or expanding into new territories exceed the revenue they can generate.

In this case, while the percentage of loss slightly decreased, in terms of raw dollars, it did not. During 2011, 2012, and 2013, the annual loss continued to increase, and it was in 2013 that many investors became anxious. By this point, there were also bank loans and other forms of debt.

In 2014, Musify's entry into Latin America posed some unique challenges. For example, when penetrating denser markets, there was a considerable increase in users, but these were markets with far less purchasing power. As a result, for every premium account, Musify earned between $4 and $5 on average per month, compared to the $8-$9 it was earning before this expansion.

However, the sheer number of users began to balance out operational and expansion costs. From 2013 to 2014, the loss percentage improved by 4 points, and for the first time since its inception, the annual financial loss was less than the previous year. Although the loss was still large, and the accumulated investment even larger, investors were more at ease because the financials were improving, and the project's vision was much clearer. At this point, many partners felt it was only a matter of time before the company began turning a profit.

It's unusual for a startup's financial losses to reach the levels that Musify's did, and it's believed that the real numbers may be different. Some investment or tax strategies may have been employed, so what we see might not be entirely real. The figures presented here have been adjusted by me for the sake of clarity and illustration, but in general, they closely resemble reality.

During this phase, when Musify successfully entered the American market and made its first steps in Asia, they faced their biggest legal challenges regarding music rights. Although contracts with record labels provided some protection, artists found "legal loopholes" that allowed them to apply official pressure against Musify. The company's lack of profitability meant they were in no position to renegotiate terms or payouts per stream.

In some ways, and this is my perception, I believe that the legal issues with artists, record labels, and their representatives pushed Musify to accelerate its global market expansion. They seemed to realize that, with a large enough market share, artists would have little recourse—even if legal actions went against them. Furthermore, this expansion would provide Musify with greater capital to operate and more leverage over creators.

The reality was that most of the artists and legal actions opposing Musify were demanding higher payouts per stream and other related benefits. However, almost none of them were asking to have their music removed from the platform. That is to say, Musify had become so widespread and prevalent that composers and performers themselves didn't want to be left out. Removing their music felt like professional suicide.

Given this legal interpretation, Musify decided to press forward without making any changes. At this point, the legal team became crucial because, although they had hoped protection would come through contracts with the record labels, once they saw that artists had no intention of leaving, their position shifted dramatically: any artist who requested their content be removed would have their request honored immediately.

This, which would have been impossible 5-6 years earlier, was the result of their significant market share by this point. Additionally, this policy gave Musify a strong legal argument that no one was forced to have their music on the platform, even under contracts with record labels, and that copyrights were protected. Moreover, artists had the freedom to accept or reject Musify's offer regarding payment per stream.

While it might seem that the legal issue isn't important enough to warrant so much attention, it was a key part of a strategy that ensured Musify's future survival. Without this legal maneuvering, the service would not exist today. I'm not arguing whether the payouts to artists were fair (or not), I'm simply pointing out that this is how it happened—and continues to happen. It's also important to highlight that the service's price point wasn't arbitrary. There was already a clear public perception regarding subscription costs for streaming services, and a 300-400% price hike would have been equally catastrophic for Musify (and for many users).

Many artists did request the removal of their catalog from the platform, and as per company policy, their requests were immediately granted. Most of these artists later returned to Musify on their own accord, while others faded into obscurity due to not being part of the platform. There were some, however, with substantial fame and strong fan bases who remained outside Musify without any significant professional catastrophe. One of the most famous examples is a country music artist with great fame in the U.S. and worldwide—who I won't name, but let's call him **Bart Grooks**. Some of his works have recently been uploaded to Musify, but it's unclear whether they are officially his. The reality is that his catalog is still absent.

Also, it's important to note that in 2011, with the introduction of ad-supported accounts, user numbers skyrocketed. However, ad sales weren't as easy as expected, and prices were high for the benefits offered to advertisers, which they would only realize later. Nonetheless, by 2015, they generated $43 million USD in revenue from ads, a significant increase from $16 million USD in 2012.

Here are the numbers for this important phase:

2011

- **Strategy**: Free version with ads
- **Market Reaction**: User surge
- **Differentiator**: Free with ads
- **Territory Covered**: Europe, U.S.
- **Number of ad-supported accounts**: 1,233,550
- **Number of premium accounts**: 1,843,444
- **Total accounts**: 3,076,994
- **Average monthly revenue per ad account**: $1.4
- **Average monthly revenue per premium account**: $8
- **Approximate total monthly revenue**: $16,474,522

- **Approximate annual revenue of Musify**: $197,694,264
- **Profit/Loss**: -$57,331,337
- **Investment Status**: -$129,549,931

2012

- **Strategy**: Global label agreements
- **Market Reaction**: Growth
- **Differentiator**: Larger catalog
- **Territory Covered**: Europe, U.S.
- **Number of ad-supported accounts**: 2,343,745
- **Number of premium accounts**: 2,343,745
- **Total accounts**: 4,740,222
- **Average monthly revenue per ad account**: $1
- **Average monthly revenue per premium account**: $8.8
- **Approximate total monthly revenue**: $23,432,744
- **Approximate annual revenue of Musify**: $281,192,932
- **Profit/Loss**: -$64,674,374
- **Investment Status**: -$194,224,305

2013

- **Strategy**: Mobile app/Version
- **Market Reaction**: Demand generation
- **Differentiator**: Mobile
- **Territory Covered**: Europe, U.S., Canada
- **Number of ad-supported accounts**: 3,453,116
- **Number of premium accounts**: 3,115,420
- **Total accounts**: 7,568,536
- **Average monthly revenue per ad account**: $1.1

- **Average monthly revenue per premium account**: $9.68
- **Approximate total monthly revenue**: $35,055,696
- **Approximate annual revenue of Musify**: $420,668,354
- **Profit/Loss**: -$92,547,038
- **Investment Status**: -$286,771,343

2014

- **Strategy**: Full expansion. Social features
- **Market Reaction**: Massive growth
- **Differentiator**: Integration with social networks
- **Territory Covered**: Europe, North America, Latin America
- **Number of ad-supported accounts**: 8,460,919
- **Number of premium accounts**: 4,050,046
- **Total accounts**: 12,511,966
- **Average monthly revenue per ad account**: $1.21
- **Average monthly revenue per premium account**: $5.3
- **Approximate total monthly revenue**: $31,702,959
- **Approximate annual revenue of Musify**: $380,435,506
- **Profit/Loss**: -$68,478,391
- **Investment Status**: -$355,249,734

2015

- **Strategy**: **Connect**
- **Market Reaction**: Adoption through desire
- **Differentiator**: Remote control
- **Territory Covered**: Europe, Americas, Asia

- **Number of ad-supported accounts**: 16,075,747
- **Number of premium accounts**: 5,265,060
- **Total accounts**: 21,340,807
- **Average monthly revenue per ad account**: $1.19
- **Average monthly revenue per premium account**: $4.6
- **Approximate total monthly revenue**: $43,349,417
- **Approximate annual revenue of Musify**: $520,193,001
- **Profit/Loss**: -$57,221,230
- **Investment Status**: -$412,470,964

Phase 4: Breakthrough Phase

This is where all the magic happened. Losses were already consistently shrinking, and sales increased year over year. Even so, the total numbers were still in the red. Musify had accumulated more than $400 million in losses, and the financial problem was immense.

Do you remember when I mentioned the cornered animal? This was the corner. They had $400 million on their back and an uncertain future. It's true that this story eventually turns into a success, but standing at that moment must have been very difficult. Moving forward meant more investment, and quitting meant a historic loss.

In the end, the statistics and trends told investors they were on the right path. The new challenges and the vision of their leader, combined with the team's commitment, were much clearer. The action plan was already in place, and everyone involved held firm.

By early 2016, they had already begun gathering the initial data. According to my calculations, from 2014–2015, they completed the market research (which we talked about in some detail), and they were ready to launch the recommendation features.

The first phase of personalization, which wasn't as advanced but still a major innovation for the market, began operating in 2016. The system's ability to suggest music was a big hit, helping Musify expand into the remaining territories, except for China and a few select countries, which they didn't intend to enter—either due to known political-commercial barriers or because the countries' network infrastructure made them untargetable markets.

In addition to the recommendation lists, the original playlists (not personalized) also gained traction. In 2016, Musify added around 15 million new users. It's true that most were for ad-supported accounts, but even so, market penetration was almost total, and the number of accounts signaled a favorable turn for the business.

That year, they came close to breaking even. The global balance showed a loss of just 2%, a 9-point reduction in losses, and the financial loss was "only" $16 million. While they were still deeply in the red, the trend was clearly positive.

Throughout 2016, they perfected the recommendation system. But all of that year, it was only available to users with paid accounts. In 2017, they released the full algorithm. However, what really happened that year was that the initial recommendation phase did the groundwork and allowed them to capture a much larger market. The number of users almost doubled, and premium accounts grew by over 300%. It became obvious that their innovations and differentiation strategies were sufficient to aim for market leadership. Additionally, a large portion of the global population now understood the music streaming product. Brand awareness and recognition had completed their penetration phase, and the work was now about continuing growth and launching periodic innovations. These innovations didn't need to be as radical or complex as those that got them here: **Personalizing music for every user**.

Fully aware that the remaining territorial markets wouldn't open in the near or medium term, Musify essentially suspended all efforts to expand into new countries. This helped reduce the advertising and infrastructure costs they had regularly incurred, and they managed to turn their negative margin of -2% into a positive 8%. The growth of ad-supported accounts, paid accounts, and the reduction in operating costs led the company to generate over $1.5 billion in revenue, with a gross margin of 9%, producing operating profits of more than $137 million.

The cumulative investment loss shrank drastically from -$428 million to -$291 million. They paid off loans, and for the first time, investors saw returns on their risks. Here, I want to take a moment to recognize both the operators and the investors. Enduring 14 years of losses in an emerging business took extraordinary vision. I know there were difficult moments, but the analysis and projection skills they all showed to reach this point are worth highlighting.

In the following year, there was no need to do anything radically different. They reduced costs a bit more and nearly doubled their total users again. This time, the percentage growth was similar for both ad-supported and paid accounts. Musify began accepting the decrease in revenue per account. Each ad-supported account generated an average of just $0.50, and each paid account about $4.1. The key now was no longer individual revenue but massive scale.

Musify generated $2.7 billion in 2018 with a 9% gross margin, producing operating profits of over $240 million. The accumulated investment loss was reduced to $50 million—almost 10% of the worst year's total loss. Investors had practically recovered all of their investment, and in addition, they now had a large, profitable, and scalable business in their hands. The remaining $50 million could easily be covered through bank loans, and with a sales forecast of $3 billion, that $50 million no longer seemed significant.

Here are the numbers for the three years contained in the breakthrough phase (again, while these figures are close to reality, the purpose of this exercise is to illustrate the process and its changes):

2016

- **Strategy**: Algorithm creation
- **Market Reaction**: Growth
- **Differentiator**: Basic personalization
- **Territory Covered**: Global except for barriers
- **Number of ad-supported accounts**: 30,543,919
- **Number of premium accounts**: 6,844,579
- **Total accounts**: 37,388,498
- **Average monthly revenue per ad account**: $1.1
- **Average monthly revenue per premium account**: $5.06

- **Approximate total monthly revenue**: $68,231,879
- **Approximate annual revenue of Musify**: $818,782,542
- **Profit/Loss**: -$16,375,651
- **Investment Status**: -$428,846,615

2017

- **Strategy**: Algorithm launch
- **Market Reaction**: Boom
- **Differentiator**: Advanced personalization
- **Territory Covered**: Global except for barriers
- **Number of ad-supported accounts**: 50,250,250
- **Number of premium accounts**: 22,640,400
- **Total accounts**: 75,890,650
- **Average monthly revenue per ad account**: $0.9
- **Average monthly revenue per premium account**: $4.2
- **Approximate total monthly revenue**: $143,014,905
- **Approximate annual revenue of Musify**: $1,716,178,860
- **Profit/Loss**: $137,294,309
- **Investment Status**: -$291,552,306

2018

- **Strategy**: Integration with other services and apps
- **Market Reaction**: Continuous growth
- **Differentiator**: Open ecosystem
- **Territory Covered**: Global except for barriers
- **Number of ad-supported accounts**: 98,125,325
- **Number of premium accounts**: 42,568,102
- **Total accounts**: 140,693,427

- **Average monthly revenue per ad account**: $0.9
- **Average monthly revenue per premium account**: $4.2
- **Approximate total monthly revenue**: $140,014,905
- **Approximate annual revenue of Musify**: $2,683,102,568
- **Profit/Loss**: $241,479,231
- **Investment Status**: -$50,073,045

Phase 5: Consolidation Phase

This phase covers the period from 2018 to 2023, where consolidation was fully achieved. To me, and I stress this point, **Phase 4** is what truly turned Musify into the giant it is today. **Phase 5** was much simpler tactically and in terms of innovation; by 2023, the market wasn't demanding much more than what they were already getting. In fact, the majority of users don't fully take advantage of the many features the platform offers.

That said, I must acknowledge that the operational side must have been very, very complicated. The complexity of running a global machine just 12 years after its founding shouldn't be taken for granted. It's true that the major concerns—finances, technology, and market growth—had been addressed in previous phases, but with the brand's global consolidation came operational and infrastructure challenges, particularly without new investments. Furthermore, Musify faced significant attacks from governments, platforms, competitors, and even their own "suppliers" (the artists and labels), making this phase equally challenging.

2019 confirmed the project's positive trajectory: user numbers increased, sales grew, margins expanded, and for the first time since its founding, Musify's debt was above zero. After years in which innovation-driven intelligence dominated the leadership's minds, **2019** was marked by commercial intelligence and growth strategies.

New "premium" plans were introduced, including family packages and **student** discounts. For example, they offered a **couples' package** that not only gave two users a combo deal but also allowed some level of relationship between the two accounts. The **student plan** offered appropriate discounts, which attracted many new users. And let's not forget the **family plans**, where not only could the couple be included, but also their children. While this move didn't bring many new paid accounts, it significantly increased the number of users. At this point, revenue growth was well underway, but Musify still sought to expand its market share.

Naturally, the average revenue per account dropped significantly, but this was always under Musify's control. By 2019, their market share of **music/streaming/premium services** had reached 20% worldwide, solidifying their market dominance. Sales in 2019 surpassed **$3.75 billion**.

For **2020**, Musify had big plans for market strategies. Their objectives were to attract new users, convert free users into paid subscribers, and use simple information to help users understand the platform's advanced features, aiming to foster widespread loyalty.

Now, what do you remember about **2020**? Exactly, a **global pandemic**. Everyone knows this event was a turning point in human history. We know that many people died, others were left with severe aftereffects, and countless businesses were severely impacted, with many forced to close due to the challenges of a global catastrophe. But we also know that a small handful of people and businesses financially benefited and experienced significant growth.

Musify was one of those beneficiaries. Looking back, if they had taken a couple more years to consolidate, they might not have had this boom and market solidification. But everything happened **just in time**. At the moment of brand consolidation, 70% of the working population was at home, glued to a computer. The use (and overuse) of music became almost a basic necessity, so the news for Musify was all positive.

I believe every great business benefits from one or two strokes of **luck**. Global behavior changed completely, and online interactions between people saw a disproportionate increase. This favored several companies in the "Internet of Things" space, like the video call company zzzuuumm. But in addition to what I've already mentioned, this rise in online interactions led people to use new tools—or old tools in new ways.

Part of this new behavior included **sharing** things with colleagues, friends, and family. Chat apps became more popular, and even phone calls saw a resurgence (I know, not exactly innovative, but it happened). In Musify's case, the feature to **share songs or playlists** saw a **300%** increase, and with that, market penetration became unstoppable. People across much of the world began assuming everyone used Musify, so they shared a link to a song, artist, album, or playlist. Those receiving these links, who weren't Musify users, became users out of curiosity, discovery, guilt, or resignation.

This led to **70 million new users** in 2020, **90 million** in 2021 (still as an obvious result of the COVID-19 pandemic). Without the pandemic, in 2022, they gained **122 million** new users, and in 2023, **160 million**. The brand, platform, and leadership were being consolidated with increasing clarity. As I write this, there seems to be no force capable of stopping the Musify project, and in fact, while writing, I'm listening to my "new music" playlist.

The surge in sales, driven by demand rather than supply, led the company to focus on **maintaining** and **growing their technological infrastructure**, making Musify not just a good product, but a highly **reliable service**, with almost **zero outages worldwide**. Very few companies can boast this level of reliability—neither the big search engines, social networks, chat platforms, nor banks have a similar track record.

This situation "pushed" Musify to significantly reduce its focus on innovation, though its team continued working on occasional new features. In this final phase, Musify made adjustments to advanced functions, increased its focus on **exclusive content**, and launched **video podcasts** and traditional podcasts. Even with a slowdown in innovation, personalization kept advancing in detail for each user. Moreover, their catalog was practically complete and kept growing, nearly 100% driven by artist demand. It seems that the brand's leadership is now consolidated and guaranteed for several more years.

Here are the numbers for this final phase:

2019

- **Strategy**: Student and family packages
- **Market Reaction**: Explosion of subscriptions
- **Differentiator**: Diversified offers
- **Territory Covered**: Global except for barriers
- **Number of ad-supported accounts**: 130,506,682
- **Number of premium accounts**: 59,595,343
- **Total accounts**: 190,102,025
- **Average monthly revenue per ad account**: $0.5
- **Average monthly revenue per premium account**: $4.15
- **Approximate total monthly revenue**: $312,574,014
- **Approximate annual revenue of Musify**: $3,750,888,165
- **Profit/Loss**: $375,088,816
- **Investment Status**: $325,015,741

2020

- **Strategy**: Adjustments to monetization and advanced features
- **Market Reaction**: High use during pandemic
- **Differentiator**: New features
- **Territory Covered**: Global except for barriers
- **Number of ad-supported accounts**: 173,573,887
- **Number of premium accounts**: 83,433,480
- **Total accounts**: 257,007,367

- **Average monthly revenue per ad account**: $0.5
- **Average monthly revenue per premium account**: $4.15
- **Approximate total monthly revenue**: $433,035,885
- **Approximate annual revenue of Musify**: $5,196,430,624
- **Profit/Loss**: $571,607,369
- **Investment Status**: $898,623,110

2021

- **Strategy**: Exclusive content
- **Market Reaction**: Expansion through exclusive content
- **Differentiator**: Exclusivity and podcasts
- **Territory Covered**: Global except for barriers
- **Number of ad-supported accounts**: 230,853,270
- **Number of premium accounts**: 116,806,872
- **Total accounts**: 347,660,142
- **Average monthly revenue per ad account**: $0.5
- **Average monthly revenue per premium account**: $4.2
- **Approximate total monthly revenue**: $600,175,153
- **Approximate annual revenue of Musify**: $7,202,101,841
- **Profit/Loss**: $864,252,221
- **Investment Status**: $1,760,875,331

2022

- **Strategy**: Expansion of content and emerging markets
- **Market Reaction**: Stability

- **Differentiator**: Advanced personalization
- **Territory Covered**: Global except for barriers
- **Number of ad-supported accounts**: 307,034,849
- **Number of premium accounts**: 163,529,621
- **Total accounts**: 470,564,470
- **Average monthly revenue per ad account**: $0.5
- **Average monthly revenue per premium account**: $4.2
- **Approximate total monthly revenue**: $840,341,831
- **Approximate annual revenue of Musify**: $10,084,101,997
- **Profit/Loss**: $1,210,092,237
- **Investment Status**: $2,970,967,568

2023

- **Strategy**: Expansion of content and emerging markets
- **Market Reaction**: Stability
- **Differentiator**: Advanced personalization
- **Territory Covered**: Global except for barriers
- **Number of ad-supported accounts**: 394,685,322
- **Number of premium accounts**: 236,789,314
- **Total accounts**: 631,474,636
- **Average monthly revenue per ad account**: $0.5
- **Average monthly revenue per premium account**: $4.2
- **Approximate total monthly revenue**: $1,191,857,780
- **Approximate annual revenue of Musify**: $14,302,293,358
- **Profit/Loss**: $1,787,786,670
- **Investment Status**: $4,758,754,238

It seems like a great success story at this point, a huge business. However, don't forget all the hardships they went through at the beginning, the level of intelligence, innovation, and execution required to truly turn the tide. But most importantly, I want you to remember the key takeaway: **personalization**.

Summary Tables

Strategy Table

Year	Strategy	Market Reaction to the Strategy	Differentiator	Territory Covered
2004-2007	Initial Investment	N/A	N/A	N/A
2008	Concept Creation. Fastest Online Player. Launch	Curiosity	Playback speed	Cuesia
2009	Initial Expansion to Europe	Initial Interest	Speed and expanded catalog	Ureopa (Scotland, UK, Spain)
2010	Platform Growth, Launch in More Countries	Rapid Adoption	Expanded music catalog	Ureopa
2011	Introduction of Free Version with Ads	User Surge	Free version with ads	Ureopa and United States
2012	First Deals with Major Record Labels	Exponential Growth	Large music catalog	Ureopa and United States
2013	Introduction of Mobile Version	High Demand	Mobile and multi-device	Ureopa, United States, and Canada
2014	Expansion to More Markets and New Social Features	Strong Growth	Integration with social networks	Ureopa, North America, and Latin America
2015	Launch of Musify Connect	Increased Adoption	Remote control across devices	America, Ureopa, and parts of Asia
2016	Market Data Identification and Advanced	Strong Growth	Data-driven personalization	Global (except some markets)

Year	Strategy	Market Reaction to the Strategy	Differentiator	Territory Covered
	Algorithm Creation			
2017	Algorithm Launch	Market Boom	Music personalization	Global (except China and some markets)
2018	Integration with Other Services and Apps	Continued Growth	Open ecosystem	Global
2019	Premium Offers for Families and Students	Subscription Explosion	Diversified offers	Global
2020	Monetization Adjustments and Advanced Features	High Use During Pandemic	New features	Global
2021	Exclusive Content and Video Podcast Launch	Content Expansion	Exclusivity and video podcasts	Global
2022	Content Expansion and Emerging Markets	Stability	Advanced personalization	85% of the world
2023	Leadership	Stability	Personalization	85% of the world

Users and Accounts Table

Year	Ad-Supported Accounts	Premium Accounts	Total Accounts	Avg. Monthly Revenue per Ad Account (USD)	Avg. Monthly Revenue per Premium Account (USD)
2004-2007	N/A	N/A	N/A	N/A	N/A
2008	0	211,000	211,000	$0.00	$8.00
2009	0	419,568	419,568	$0.00	$8.00
2010	0	1,433,833	1,433,833	$0.00	$8.00
2011	1,233,550	1,843,444	3,076,994	$1.40	$8.00
2012	2,343,745	2,396,477	4,740,222	$1.00	$8.80
2013	4,453,116	3,115,420	7,568,536	$1.10	$9.68
2014	8,460,919	4,050,046	12,510,966	$1.21	$5.30
2015	16,075,747	5,265,060	21,340,807	$1.19	$4.60
2016	30,543,919	6,844,579	37,388,498	$1.10	$5.06
2017	53,250,250	22,640,400	75,890,650	$0.90	$4.20
2018	98,125,325	42,568,102	140,693,427	$0.50	$4.10
2019	130,506,682	59,595,343	190,102,025	$0.50	$4.15
2020	173,573,887	83,433,480	257,007,367	$0.50	$4.15
2021	230,853,270	116,806,872	347,660,142	$0.50	$4.15
2022	307,034,849	163,529,621	470,564,470	$0.50	$4.20
2023	394,685,322	236,789,314	631,474,636	$0.50	$4.20

Revenue and Investment Table

Year	Approx. Monthly Revenue Musify (USD)	Annual Revenue	Profit/Loss	Investment Status
2004-2007	N/A	N/A	-$5,000,000	-$5,000,000
2008	$1,688,000	$20,256,000	-$7,697,280	-$12,697,280
2009	$3,356,544	$40,278,528	-$14,097,485	-$26,794,765
2010	$11,470,664	$137,647,968	-$45,423,829	-$72,218,594
2011	$16,474,522	$197,694,264	-$57,331,337	-$129,549,931

Year	Approx. Monthly Revenue Musify (USD)	Annual Revenue	Profit/Loss	Investment Status
2012	$23,432,744	$281,192,932	-$64,674,374	-$194,224,305
2013	$35,055,696	$420,668,354	-$92,547,038	-$286,771,343
2014	$31,702,959	$380,435,506	-$68,478,391	-$355,249,734
2015	$43,349,417	$520,193,001	-$57,221,230	-$412,470,964
2016	$68,231,879	$818,782,542	-$16,375,651	-$428,846,615
2017	$143,014,905	$1,716,178,860	$137,294,309	-$291,552,306
2018	$223,591,881	$2,683,102,568	$241,479,231	-$50,073,075
2019	$312,574,014	$3,750,888,165	$375,088,816	$325,015,741
2020	$433,035,885	$5,196,430,624	$571,607,369	$896,623,110
2021	$600,175,153	$7,202,101,841	$864,252,221	$1,760,875,331
2022	$840,341,831	$10,084,101,977	$1,210,092,237	$2,970,967,568
2023	$1,191,857,780	$14,302,293,358	$1,787,786,670	$4,758,754,238

The Example

Here, we will look at examples of personalization that align with Musify's strategy. It doesn't mean they are inspired by it, or came after it. What I want to demonstrate through these two stories is the capability a company can have to personalize its offering, even if they are not technology companies.

I understand that the examples I'm going to mention come from large brands with enormous budgets. However, I do so because I want you, as the reader, to be familiar with the brand and to make sense of the example. If I were to use a small, unknown brand, you'd likely lose interest quickly!

What I hope is that through these examples, you can see how an idea can break out of the traditional box and transform into something that resonates incredibly well with customers. Let's begin:

Shoes for You

This first example is about shoes… well, sneakers, really… or, all kinds of footwear. I'll refer to it as "Kine."

Kine and the Personalization Revolution: "Kine made for U"

Since its humble beginnings in 1964, Kine has been a pioneer in the footwear and sportswear industry. What started as a small company selling imported shoes from Japan has grown into a global powerhouse that not only dominates the sportswear market but also sets trends in innovation, marketing, and more recently, in personalization. In a world where unique, custom-made experiences are becoming increasingly important, Kine has been a visionary by integrating personalization as one of its cornerstones with the launch of its platform, "Kine made for U."

Imagine walking into a Kine store or visiting their website. You don't just pick a pair of shoes from dozens of pre-set models and colors. With Kine made for U, you can design your own shoes from scratch, choosing every aspect—from the materials to the colors, textures, and final details. This approach allows customers to not only buy a product but become co-creators of it. Kine has understood something fundamental: in the age of hyper-personalization, what consumers value most is the ability to express their individuality through the products they purchase.

The Evolution Towards Personalization

The evolution of Kine made for U (previously known as KineiD) began in 1999, long before personalization became a trend. At that time, the idea of allowing customers to personalize their shoes seemed risky from both logistical and operational perspectives. However, Kine realized that the future of brands was not only in offering quality products but in providing unique, personalized experiences that established a deeper connection between the consumer and the brand.

Initially, the KineiD program was limited to a few models and customization options. Customers could select from a reduced range of colors and materials, allowing them to make small tweaks to their sneakers. However, as technology advanced and interest in personalization grew, Kine expanded its options, allowing users to adjust every detail of their shoes—from the sole to the logo, to the laces and stitches. What started as an attractive feature for fashion and sports lovers soon became one of the brand's greatest strengths.

Empowering the Consumer

The true impact of Kine made for U goes far beyond offering customizable sneakers. By allowing customers to design their own products, Kine transformed the traditional relationship between consumer and brand. The customer is no longer just a passive recipient of what Kine decides to make; now, they have a say in the creation of their own product. This level of personal involvement not only increases the perceived value of the item but also creates a stronger emotional connection with the brand.

The process of designing sneakers through Kine made for U is an experience in itself. The customer has full control over the creation of their product, choosing from hundreds of combinations of colors, materials, and features. At the end of the process, what the customer receives is not just a pair of shoes but a tangible manifestation of their own style and personality. This ability to express individuality has been key to attracting consumers who value exclusivity and differentiation in a market saturated with mass-produced products.

Data and Trends: The Key to Success

Kine made for U has also allowed the company to gain valuable insights into its consumers' individual preferences. By collecting data on the most selected colors, materials, and designs, Kine can refine its production and marketing strategies. This feedback not only helps optimize operations but also positions them as trendsetters. In fact, some of the most popular designs on the platform have directly influenced the standard product lines the company launches each season.

Kine's strategy of collecting data on users' customization patterns gives it a significant competitive edge. As the company gathers more information on customers' design preferences, it can anticipate market trends and develop products that respond directly to emerging demands. This data-driven approach has allowed Kine to not only stay at the forefront of the sports footwear industry but also solidify its position as a leader in innovation.

The Fusion of Physical and Digital

The success of this initiative lies in Kine's ability to seamlessly integrate technology with the customer experience. What might have been a simple additional option at other brands becomes an essential part of the brand's identity at Kine made for U. The platform is designed to be intuitive and accessible, allowing anyone to design their own shoes without needing technical knowledge. Additionally, the integration of high-quality 3D graphics allows users to visualize their design in real-time, giving them an accurate representation of what the final product will look like.

Kine understands that the customer experience goes beyond purchasing a physical product. That's why it has invested heavily in creating a digital platform that allows consumers to interact with the brand in a meaningful way. The ability to visualize the personalized design in 3D not only enhances the user experience but also increases the likelihood that the customer will complete the purchase by providing an accurate representation of the final product.

Moreover, Kine has integrated its physical stores with the Kine made for U platform, allowing customers to visit the stores and receive personalized assistance in designing their footwear. This fusion of physical and digital not only creates a richer shopping experience but also strengthens the relationship between the customer and the brand.

Personalization and Athletic Performance

The true power of Kine made for U does not lie solely in aesthetic customization. The platform also allows athletes to design products that perfectly fit their physical needs. For example, runners can choose shoes with soles appropriate for the type of terrain they train on, while basketball players can select designs that offer greater ankle support. This approach has allowed Kine to stand out not only in the sportswear market but also in the high-performance products sector.

For many athletes, personalization is not just a matter of style but of functionality. Custom-designed shoes allow athletes to adjust every aspect of the footwear to maximize their performance on the field or track. This ability to tailor the product to the user's specific needs has been crucial for Kine, which has managed to attract both professional and amateur athletes by offering a level of personalization that goes beyond the superficial.

Expanding to New Product Categories

Although personalization began with footwear, Kine made for U has expanded its offerings to include other products such as apparel and sports accessories. Now, consumers can design their own shirts, pants, and backpacks, allowing them to create a sports kit that is not only functional but also reflects their personal style. By offering this expanded range of customizable products, Kine has managed to meet the growing demand for personalized shopping experiences across all areas.

This approach has been particularly popular among sports teams and fans, who can customize their team equipment, from colors to logos. This ability to personalize for groups has allowed Kine to position itself as the preferred provider for many sports teams worldwide, from youth leagues to professional club

Impact on Customer Loyalty

Another key aspect of the success of Kine made for U is its ability to generate loyalty among consumers. By allowing customers to actively participate in the creation process, Kine fosters a deeper and longer-lasting relationship. When someone designs their own pair of sneakers, they're not just buying a product; they're buying an experience, a tangible manifestation of their style and preferences. This emotional bond is hard to break, making these customers much more likely to return and continue purchasing from the brand.

In fact, it has been shown that customers who personalize their products have a higher repeat purchase rate and a greater propensity to recommend the brand to others. By feeling part of the creation process, consumers develop a sense of belonging and loyalty to the brand that goes beyond what a traditional purchase can offer.

Economic Advantages of Personalization

From a business perspective, personalization has not only been a marketing tool for Kine but also a revenue-generating strategy. Customized products often come with a higher price tag than standard models, allowing the company to increase its profit margins without having to compete on price. Additionally, the longer production times associated with personalized products have not been a barrier; in fact, many consumers are willing to wait weeks to receive their custom-designed pair of shoes. This demonstrates the perceived value that personalized products hold and the level of satisfaction they generate.

Conclusion: A Paradigm Shift

In summary, Kine made for U is not just a personalization strategy; it is a paradigm shift in how brands can connect with their customers. By empowering consumers to become co-creators, Kine has managed to transcend the traditional model of product sales and create a platform that not only generates revenue but also reinforces the emotional relationship between the brand and the customer. In an increasingly competitive world, where differentiation is key, Kine has demonstrated that personalization is not just an option—it's a necessity.

This approach has not only transformed the customer experience but also redefined how brands can leverage technology and data to offer products tailored to the unique needs and desires of their consumers. Kine made for U is proof that personalization is the future of retail, and Kine, as always, is leading the way.

A soda with your name

Now let's talk about a company that makes soft drinks. You probably have an idea of who it might be, but for these purposes, we'll call it "LolaLoca."

Lolaloca and Mass Personalization: "Split a Loke"

Throughout its history, Lolaloca has been one of the most recognized and beloved brands worldwide. Since its creation in 1886, it has maintained a consistent and familiar image associated with happiness, friendship, and celebration. However, Lolaloca's true genius doesn't lie solely in its product but in its ability to reinvent itself without losing its essence. In 2011, the brand launched one of the most successful campaigns in its history: "Split a Loke," an initiative that transformed how consumers interacted with the product by introducing an unprecedented level of personalization in the mass consumption market.

The Birth of "Split a Loke"

The "Split a Loke" campaign began in Australia in 2011 and was a bold experiment to revitalize the brand in an increasingly competitive and saturated market. The concept behind the campaign was simple yet powerful: replacing Lolaloca's iconic logo on its packaging with common names. Instead of seeing the traditional red and white label with the brand's logo, consumers would find cans and bottles with popular names printed on them, inviting them to "share a Lolaloca" with friends, family, or even strangers.

This small change in packaging had a huge impact. The idea of finding your own name or that of someone close to you on a bottle of Lolaloca resonated deeply with consumers, who no longer saw the product as just a drink but as a personal and meaningful object. This level of mass personalization was revolutionary for a brand that had maintained a very homogeneous approach for over a century. With "Split a Loke," Lolaloca didn't just adapt its product to the individual; it created a new consumption experience that encouraged social interaction and personal connection.

A Global Cultural Impact

What started as a local campaign in Australia quickly expanded globally. The success was such that by 2013, Lolaloca launched the campaign in more than 70 countries, including key markets like the United States, the United Kingdom, Brazil, China, and Mexico. Each country adapted the list of names to the most popular ones in their region, giving the campaign a local touch while maintaining its global appeal.

The key to the success of "Split a Loke" was that it wasn't just about finding a name on a bottle; it was about sharing moments and connections. Lolaloca had always positioned itself as a brand that brought people together, but this campaign allowed them to do so in a tangible way. The act of finding a bottle with a friend or family member's name and gifting it to them became a symbol of affection and appreciation. Suddenly, buying a Lolaloca wasn't just about quenching your thirst—it became a way to connect with others.

The Power of Personalization in Mass Consumption

What made the "Split a Loke" campaign so innovative was that it introduced personalization into a mass consumption market. Traditionally, personalization was associated with premium products or exclusive services where customers would pay extra to have something custom-made. However, Lolaloca demonstrated that it was possible to bring personalization to a mass level without significantly increasing production costs.

The process behind the campaign required complex logistics in printing and distribution. Bottling plants had to adapt their production lines to print thousands of different names on the bottles, which presented considerable organizational and efficiency challenges. Nevertheless, Lolaloca managed to overcome these obstacles and maintain consistency across all markets, showcasing its ability to innovate in supply chain management.

This mass personalization strategy also allowed Lolaloca to stand out in a highly competitive market where consumer attention is fiercely contested. By offering a product that felt unique to each individual, the brand generated greater consumer engagement and loyalty. Additionally, the fact that consumers could share their experiences on social media helped amplify the campaign's reach, generating a huge amount of free publicity.

The Social Media Era and Viral Effect

One of the most powerful aspects of the "Split a Loke" campaign was how it took advantage of the rise of social media. In 2011, platforms like Facebook, Twitter, and Instagram were already in full swing, and Lolaloca capitalized on this trend brilliantly. Consumers weren't just buying Lolaloca for the product itself, but to show on social media that they had found their name or that of someone close to them on a bottle. This viral effect generated millions of posts and shares, greatly amplifying the campaign's reach without requiring Lolaloca to invest further in traditional advertising.

Personalization didn't just occur in stores but also in the digital realm. Lolaloca allowed consumers to create virtual bottles with names that weren't available in stores and share them on their social media. This extended the campaign's life cycle and allowed the brand to interact with consumers in a more dynamic and personalized way. The combination of physical and digital personalization was key to keeping the campaign relevant for several years.

Moreover, Lolaloca integrated various interactive activations into events and real-time advertising campaigns. In many cities around the world, special vending machines were set up that allowed consumers to print their own name on a bottle instantly. These machines not only generated long lines of people excited to have their personalized Lolaloca, but also strengthened the emotional connection between the consumer and the brand.

Reconnecting with the Millennial Generation

One of Lolaloca's major goals with "Split a Loke" was to reconnect with the millennial generation, a demographic that had become increasingly difficult to attract with traditional marketing strategies. Millennials value authenticity, personalization, and unique experiences, and

Lolaloca was able to tap into these trends with its campaign.

The possibility of finding a bottle with their name or the name of someone important resonated strongly with this group. The personalization of products perfectly aligns with millennials' desire to feel unique and special. Additionally, the social nature of the campaign, which encouraged sharing a Lolaloca with friends or loved ones, connected with the values of connection and community that millennials prioritize.

The campaign's success also helped reverse the declining trend of soda consumption among millennials. For years, this group had shown a growing preference for healthier options such as bottled water, natural juices, or energy drinks. However, "Split a Loke" managed to get many millennials to reconsider Lolaloca as an attractive option—not so much for the product itself, but for the social and personalized experience it offered.

The Emotional Effect: Beyond the Product

One of the most important lessons from the "Split a Loke" campaign is that big brands can create a deeper emotional connection with their consumers by going beyond the simple product. While Lolaloca is still a soda that consumers have enjoyed for decades, the campaign introduced an emotional element that deeply resonated with its audience. By including names on the bottles, Lolaloca wasn't just selling a drink—it was selling an experience, a way to share a special moment with someone else.

Consumers began to associate Lolaloca not only with quenching their thirst but with the enjoyment of moments of human connection. The act of finding a bottle with the name of a loved one and giving it to them became a gesture of affection and attention, adding a significant emotional layer to the purchase of the product. By creating this emotional connection, Lolaloca not only boosted short-term sales but also strengthened its long-term relationship with consumers.

The Sustainability of the Campaign in the Long Term

Although the "Split a Loke" campaign was initially conceived as a limited-time promotion, its success was so significant that Lolaloca continued to launch variations of the campaign in subsequent years. In some countries, the brand expanded the list of names and introduced other personalized elements, such as nicknames, common phrases, or local terms that resonate with each culture. This flexible approach has allowed the campaign to remain fresh and relevant, even years after its initial launch.

Furthermore, Lolaloca learned from the "Split a Loke" campaign that consumers want to feel valued as individuals, even in mass markets. As a result, the brand has continued to explore other forms of personalization, not only in its products but also in its advertising campaigns and digital marketing strategies. From implementing personalized ads based on the consumer's purchase history to promotions that allow customers to interact with the brand in real-time, Lolaloca has fully embraced personalization as a key tool for staying relevant in the modern market.

A Legacy of Personalization

"Split a Loke" has left a lasting legacy not only in the history of Lolaloca but in global marketing. The campaign demonstrated that even the largest and most established brands can innovate and find new, exciting ways to connect with their consumers. Additionally, it highlighted the importance of personalization in a world where consumers increasingly demand experiences that are relevant to them as individuals.

Today, personalization is a fundamental strategy in many industries, from fashion to technology, and Lolaloca has been one of the pioneers in demonstrating how this approach can be scaled globally. "Split a Loke" didn't just change the perception of the brand; it also set a precedent for the future of personalized marketing in the mass consumption market.

The 10 Turning Points

Musify's history is full of key moments that drove its transformation from a small startup into one of the most powerful and recognized music platforms in the world. These milestones not only marked the evolution of the company but also redefined the way we consume music. In this chapter, we will explore the 10 most important turning points that changed the course of Musify's history and made it a giant in music streaming.

1. The Creation of the Fast Streaming Platform (2008)

At a time when music piracy was rampant and downloading songs via P2P networks like Napster and Limewire was slow and often illegal, Musify entered the market with a revolutionary concept: allowing users to listen to music in real-time without waiting for the file to fully download. Unlike other platforms of the time, where users had to wait endlessly to download MP3 files, Musify offered something unprecedented: music was ready to play with just one click, thanks to smooth, near-instant streaming.

This was Musify's first major differentiator. By implementing a robust infrastructure optimized for online streaming and caching, Musify achieved what many other platforms couldn't: deliver an uninterrupted music experience. This not only solved one of the biggest problems in digital music consumption at the time but also laid the foundation for its future success. Users no longer had to deal with annoying wait times or worry about storage space on their devices. Musify changed the game by making fast streaming the norm.

2. Global Expansion (2010)

After establishing itself in Ureopa, Musify decided to take a bold step: expand globally. International expansion wasn't a simple decision and was seen by many as a risk. At the time, musical tastes and copyright regulations varied widely from country to country. Moreover, each market presented unique challenges: local competition, cultural differences, and consumption habits.

However, Musify understood that its platform had the potential to transcend borders. The company conducted extensive market research to ensure its offerings were relevant in each region. For example, in Latin America, where music consumption is an integral part of the culture, Musify adjusted its catalog to include more local artists and genres, attracting a wider user base. Similarly, in Asia, they focused on partnerships with local record labels and ensured the catalog included popular music in local languages. Global expansion positioned Musify as a true global contender, opening new revenue streams and exponentially increasing its user base.

3. Introduction of the Freemium Model (2011)

In a world where music was still perceived as something easily accessible for free (legally or illegally), Musify even if tomorrow personalization no longer yields major benefits, it will still allow you to offer your products or services in the most appropriate way.

If you commit to these objectives, starting today will help you grow commercially for several years. It will prepare you for when personalization reaches its peak, and you'll be ready to apply other strategies that will be differentiators at the time.

People have asked me if there isn't another way to differentiate, and I think there isn't just one, but many. However, beyond innovation and targeting new segments, a personalization strategy will help any business organize its communication schemes, differentiation, and eventually, advanced personalization.

If you treat your customers with care and precision. If you offer them what they want, need, or believe they need. If you give them benefits. If you speak to them directly. If you show them your appreciation and interest… they will do the same for you.

The key point for me is that people are gradually understanding these processes, even if only subconsciously, and today online shopping and searching are activities not only being adopted by more people but also being used more hours per day by those who have already adopted them. Think of the major online shopping sites, web search engines, email systems, video and audio streaming platforms, and large brands' commercial websites, to name a few.

This activity results in people receiving more "personalized attention" through digital tools. Online shopping sites already personalize offers and product rankings based on users' profiles and browsing history, emails arrive with at least a basic level of differentiation (our names are included), and all streaming platforms generate recommendations in one form or another (though no one does it like Musify). Ultimately, even if they're not fully aware of it, people are being bombarded with personalization exercises that, while they may not directly relate to our business, are influencing changes in users' perceptions, habits, behaviors, and expectations—*and those users are our customers.*

This tells us that today is an excellent time to differentiate yourself through personalized strategies, but it will probably become a "must" in a few years rather than a differentiator. I'd start right away.

These two points are why I find the topic of this book so relevant. Because today is the time to start and differentiate yourself. Because today, you can compete and increase your commercial effectiveness. Because tomorrow it may become a necessity, and if you haven't started today, it will give you headaches. And because, and then ads for that same brand or its competitors "follow" you in the days after, based on your online activity.

While the standard protocol for remarketing isn't designed for exactly what I'm about to say, there has to be an adaptation here: *because people now understand how it works.*

Why does this matter? Let me explain briefly. Forty-five percent of people, and growing, now have a systematic habit of clicking on an ad that interests them and then immediately exiting to return to what they were doing. They do this with the understanding that the ad will show up again later. It's highly likely that they won't remember the brand's name, the product, or even what it was about. It was a fleeting interest they acted on without full awareness, "knowing" that the ad would reappear.

Here's a sidebar from the general topic of the book: if you're not advertising online, you're leaving money on the table, and if you're advertising online but not doing remarketing, you're wasting a large portion of your ad budget.

So, a mini-conclusion of point 1 is that standing out in today's digital world is challenging, but we have to make it happen. And,

2. **The custom communication expectation.** Yes, I know this is the theme of the book, but I want to highlight it under the premise that it will be difficult to compete with the high level of personalization already being delivered by today's digital giants.

In addition to the above, there are two points I want to highlight, which I always try to keep in mind when thinking about my business:

1. **The saturation of advertising.** People are going through a phase of adaptation when it comes to processing information. Today's advertising is extremely aggressive and robust. The flow of information is overwhelming, and the channels we use to "capture" the attention of our audiences are becoming increasingly invasive and interruptive.

Because of this, standing out—*not only from our competitors but from anyone vying for a slice of consumers' attention*—has become extremely challenging. Creativity *does* play a role, but it's not what we think. While creativity has managed to "engage" markets, it hasn't significantly moved the needle in commercial terms.

On the flip side of this issue is the fact that 80% or more of the information people receive comes from digital channels. So, when we do manage to grab their attention, it's unlikely that they have the time to fully analyze our offering. Consider that they may be checking their social media during a break, browsing their email at work, or simply being online for a purpose that has nothing to do with paying attention to an ad (unless it's a search term ad, which is a whole other animal we'll address later).

This problem has been addressed through tools like "remarketing" or "retargeting" developed and gradually refined by digital platforms. If you're not familiar with the term, remarketing is when you show interest in something (by clicking on an ad or visiting a website, for example),

Conclusion

This book has been quite a journey for its author. I had to read and study extensively, understand things that initially seemed simple but ended up being more complex than expected. I know that in the end, these kinds of books have both a romantic side and a technical side. I hope I have explained the romantic side in a coherent, enjoyable, relatable, and identifiable way, and the technical side in a structured, process-oriented, transmittable, and applicable manner.

I begin my conclusion with this paragraph because I genuinely believe that this is one of the strategies that can most easily be transferred from one business to another. It is my honest belief that any type of business can improve through personalization, whether it be in terms of their offerings, catalog, product kits or combos, or even communication. And it's clear to me that people are highly receptive to these kinds of actions.

We need to understand that we are living in a very different world than we were 10 years ago, and the forecast is that it will continue to change rapidly. If I'm pressed, I would say it may soon become unpredictable (as it already is in many aspects). Political, social, and economic instability predominates in 85-90% of the world, leading to high-profile complexities, especially in commercial conditions and the instability of market behavior.

7. **Implement technology to optimize and personalize the customer experience**:
   Use technological tools such as CRM, data analytics, or artificial intelligence to improve personalization and efficiency.
8. **Encourage customer participation**:
   Engage customers with your brand through interactive campaigns, contests, or surveys, generating engagement and relevant content.
9. **Continuously measure and adjust your strategies**:
   Monitor the performance of your campaigns, services, and products to continuously adjust and optimize your strategy.
10. **Prioritize the customer experience above all**:
    Make your customers' experience the core of your strategy, ensuring that every touchpoint with your brand is positive and memorable.

Quick Guide: Profitability Strategy with Complementary Products

1. **Develop a system to collect customer data**: Implement an efficient system to gather relevant information about your customers' behavior and preferences.
2. **Segment your audience based on collected data**: Divide your customers into groups according to their buying behavior, interests, and needs to better personalize your offerings.
3. **Personalize your offers and services**: Provide products and services tailored to each customer segment's interests, enhancing their experience and boosting sales.
4. **Build long-term relationships with customers**: Implement loyalty programs, personalize interactions, and communicate regularly with your customers to strengthen the relationship.
5. **Constantly innovate to adapt to customer needs**: Maintain a culture of continuous improvement, adjusting your products and services according to trends and changes in customer preferences.
6. **Offer an omnichannel experience**: Ensure your customers can interact with your brand seamlessly across all channels (physical and digital), ensuring a consistent experience.

Finally, the crowning moment in Musify's history came in 2020, when the company went public on the New York Stock Exchange. The IPO was the result of more than a decade of sustained growth, innovation, and strategic decision-making. This milestone not only solidified Musify as a tech giant but also provided the necessary funds to continue investing in new technologies and expanding its global presence.

The stock market debut was a reflection of investors' confidence in Musify's business model, as well as its ability to lead the music streaming industry for years to come. Despite the challenges faced by all publicly traded tech companies, Musify continued to show impressive growth, proving that its freemium model and focus on personalization remained incredibly successful.

Conclusion

Musify's history is marked by bold decisions, technological innovation, and a deep understanding of its users' needs. Through these 10 turning points, Musify has managed to transform not only the way we consume music but also how we connect with auditory content more broadly. From its focus on fast streaming and personalization to global expansion and diversification of its offerings, Musify has proven that success is not just about having a good idea but about executing it with vision and long-term strategy.

In its quest to expand its offerings and diversify its revenue streams, Musify decided to incorporate non-musical content into its platform. In 2018, they launched the option to listen to podcasts and other types of audio content, such as news and comedy shows. This was a brilliant strategy, as Musify understood that users weren't just looking for music but also other forms of auditory entertainment.

The addition of podcasts allowed Musify to compete with other audio platforms like Apple Podcasts and Stitcher and capture a share of the growing podcast market. Moreover, by diversifying its content, Musify became a comprehensive audio entertainment platform, attracting a new user base and increasing the time users spent on the platform.

9. Collaborative and Social Playlists (2019)

Musify has always been aware that music is a social experience, and in 2019, they capitalized on this by introducing collaborative playlists. This feature allowed users to create playlists with friends and family, adding a level of interaction and connection that didn't exist before.

Collaborative playlists not only increased user engagement but also fostered a sense of community within the platform. It was no longer just about listening to music alone but about sharing that experience with others. This feature also became very popular at events such as parties and gatherings, where guests could contribute to the playlist in real-time.

10. Going Public (2020)

their individual preferences. The most popular of these playlists was "Discover Weekly," a list that automatically updated every Monday with new songs tailored to the user's personal tastes.

This feature was revolutionary because it solved a common listener problem: decision fatigue. Instead of spending hours searching for new music, Musify users received personalized recommendations of exciting new songs without lifting a finger. "Discover Weekly" and other lists like "Release Radar" and "Daily Mix" became industry standards and were key to retaining users, as they kept the experience fresh and relevant.

7. The Mobile App and Offline Access (2016)

As the world became increasingly mobile, Musify couldn't afford to lag behind. The launch of its mobile app marked a significant milestone in the company's history, allowing users to access their favorite music from anywhere. But what really changed the game was the introduction of offline listening, a feature users had been requesting for years.

Offline access was especially crucial for those who traveled frequently or had limited internet access. Now, premium subscribers could download their favorite playlists and songs for offline listening. This not only improved the user experience but also boosted premium subscriptions, as offline functionality was exclusively available to paying customers.

8. Introduction of Non-Musical Content (2018)

kept users engaged with the platform but also significantly increased the time they spent on the app. The success of Musify's algorithm influenced many other tech platforms, from Netflix to Amazon, which adopted similar approaches to content personalization.

5. Partnership with Global Record Labels (2013)

Success in music streaming didn't just depend on user experience but also on agreements with major record labels. In the early days, many of these companies were reluctant to license their catalogs to streaming platforms due to fears of piracy and lost revenue. However, Musify demonstrated that online streaming could be a legitimate source of income, especially with its focus on fighting piracy.

Partnerships with global record labels marked a turning point for Musify. Not only did they dramatically increase the amount of music available on the platform, but they also allowed Musify to secure the rights to some of the world's most important artists. These alliances helped Musify differentiate itself from other platforms, most of which offered limited catalogs. By having agreements with major music names, Musify solidified its position as the leader in legal music streaming.

6. Creation of Personalized Playlists (2015)

In 2015, Musify introduced one of its most beloved features: personalized playlists. While playlists already existed on other platforms, what set Musify apart was its ability to create specific playlists for each user based on needed to find a way to attract consumers while generating sustainable revenue. The freemium model was its innovative answer. By offering a free ad-supported option and an ad-free premium version, Musify allowed users to choose how much they wanted to pay for the experience.

This model had a double advantage: on one hand, the free ad-supported version attracted millions of users who were unwilling to pay for music streaming services. On the other hand, the premium version offered an enhanced experience that, over time, enticed free users to become paying subscribers. In this way, Musify built a massive user base, generating revenue from both ads and premium subscriptions. This business model was so effective that many other platforms, from gaming apps to software services, later adopted it.

4. Development of the Personalized Recommendation Algorithm (2012)

One of the key moments that defined Musify was its focus on personalization. While other platforms focused solely on offering access to a vast music catalog, Musify went further by understanding that the real key was relevance. In 2012, they launched their personalized recommendation algorithm, a tool that analyzed users' listening habits—such as songs they repeated, genres they preferred, and times of day they usually listened to music—to recommend specific content.

This algorithm not only helped users discover new music more efficiently but also created a highly personalized musical ecosystem. The recommendations were so accurate that users felt Musify "knew their musical tastes better than they did." This deep personalization not only

www.ingramcontent.com/pod-product-compliance
Lightning Source LLC
Chambersburg PA
CBHW050324230526
45471CB00005B/2340